APPALOOSA

HORSES AND GROOMS CROSSING A RIVER. Courtesy of the Smithsonian Institution, the Freer Gallery of Art, Washington, D.C.

The theme of horses and grooms has a long tradition in Chinese painting. It dates back at least to the T'ang Dynasty (618–907 A.D.), when the painting of horses was established as a separate category of Chinese art. During succeeding centuries any artist who concerned himself with horse painting would return to such a traditional theme. Thus, even as late as the Ming Dynasty (1368–1644 A.D.), it reappears, providing an example of the significant role played by tradition in the art of China.

YELLOW JACKET. Courtesy of Greenwood Farms, San Antonio, Texas.

Coat patterns in Appaloosas seem to be at least as persistent as traditions in Chinese art. This young Appaloosa stallion might have been the model for the Ming artist who painted the scroll in the collection of the Freer Gallery of Art.

APPALOOSA

the spotted horse
in art and history

Text by FRANCIS HAINES

PUBLISHED FOR THE AMON CARTER MUSEUM
OF WESTERN ART, FORT WORTH, BY THE
UNIVERSITY OF TEXAS PRESS, AUSTIN

The Amon Carter Museum of Western Art, established under the will of the late Amon G. Carter, is concerned with the study and documentation of the American West. The program of the Museum is expressed in publications and exhibitions related to the many aspects of American Culture which find their identification as "Western." The Trustees of the Museum wish to express their appreciation to Francis Haines, author of the text, and to the many museums, libraries, and individuals who have contributed to this publication and to the exhibition upon which it is based.

MITCHELL A. WILDER, *Director*
Amon Carter Museum of Western Art

Library of Congress Catalog Card No. 63–11101
Copyright © 1963 by the Amon Carter Museum of Western Art
All Rights Reserved
Printed in the United States of America
by The Meriden Gravure Company, Meriden, Connecticut
Bound by Universal Bookbindery, Inc., San Antonio, Texas

CONTENTS

ILLUSTRATIONS

INTRODUCTION

This book and the exhibition which accompanies its publication are the product of a highly improbable collaboration between an art museum and a horse breeders' association. Such unlikely partnerships arouse the curiosity of those who care about the genesis of an idea. The proposal for an Appaloosa horse project in the world of art provided some surprise among curators and laughter in the horsey circles. It happened this way . . .

In June, 1961, I was in Fort Worth talking business with the officers of the Amon Carter Museum of Western Art. The Museum had opened a few months earlier, and I was to accept a job as its director. Killing time one evening I read a news story about the Fourteenth National Show of the Appaloosa Horse Club. If such a word as *Appaloosa* existed in my vocabulary, I was not aware of the fact. But horse shows are fun, if you aren't kin of any entrant, and I decided to join the horse fans. The only cost turned out to be taxi fare to the famed Will Rogers Coliseum, where Fort Worth stages its annual

Fat Stock Exposition. Either the ticket seller had given up or the show was planned as a benefit for the public—anyhow I went in scot-free. Someone handed me a program (free); I slipped into a box seat and took my first look at an Appaloosa horse. I seem to have seen little else in the horse world since that time, though I must confess that *Equus caballus* has never been uppermost in my mind.

The program for the National Show carried a few historical notes written by Dr. Francis Haines, historian of the Appaloosa Horse Club. This scholarly element is "Exhibit A" in the evidence that spotted horses are different; their club boasts an official historian. The story was brief: Asiatic origins, Chinese affinities, Persia, Egypt, and the rest. One picture appeared in the program —a Chinese scroll from the collections of the Fogg Museum, Harvard University. That did it! If the horse was important enough to have been the subject of one of the great artists of China, perhaps he had been depicted elsewhere. Out of this casual assumption has developed a substantial pictorial record of the spotted horse in many cultures and through many centuries. From this varied and extensive artistic product one is forced to conclude that spotted horses have been important. The reasons for this importance each man can adduce for himself—they were owned by some important people, or they are favored by artists, presumably for esthetic reasons.

The modern Appaloosa has many admirable qualities—ask any owner—but remove his unique markings and his charm wanes. My conclusion is that spotted horses have had esthetic importance for centuries, and today their popularity is established on this quality. This in no way belies their many other fine traits, but the modern horseman spends far more time showing his horses than in working them.

Dr. Haines has done more than any individual to track down information on the ancestry of the spotted horse. He brought into focus the story of the Nez Perce horse and he made possible a better understanding of the historical advance of the horse in American Indian culture from Mexico northward. Francis Haines first recognized the widespread artistic evidence which has been the basis for the research in this volume. The Museum staff and our many professional colleagues in this country and abroad have provided the multiple eyes and hands necessary to broaden the search.

The project owes a special expression of gratitude to our research associates who have secured valuable documents and pictures related to the horse. Mr. Thomas Lawton, graduate student in oriental art at Harvard University, might very well qualify with a dissertation on this animal. His contributions to our knowledge of the horse in the Orient have been outstanding. Dr. H. G. Hesslein, of Chappaqua, New York, has likewise brought a vast knowledge of art history to the horse question with astonishingly rich results. It is an interesting fact that scholars such as these seem just as susceptible to the lure of the spotted horse as does the gentleman in jeans and boots at a horse auction. Esthetics, again.

I seriously doubt that this treatment of the Appaloosa will settle all the arguments which continue among the horse fanciers. Horse genetics, fascinating as that subject is to Appaloosa owners, doesn't work its way into this story. On the other hand horse breeders would ordinarily not be searching out pictures of spotted horses on the ceiling of a fifteenth-century church in Denmark. We did—and found the results interesting. Now we find the horse people agree with us!

MITCHELL A. WILDER
*Director, Amon Carter Museum of Western Art
Fort Worth*

APPALOOSA

THE APPALOOSA HORSE IN EARLY TIMES

How the Appaloosa Was Named

A SMALL RIVER in northwestern Idaho, scarcely more than a creek, flows from a western spur of the Bitterroot Range and plunges into a narrow canyon with vertical basalt walls a few miles above its confluence with the Snake River. For many miles above the falls the little river meanders through patches of meadow land set between low hills. In late summer the scorched brown hills are in sharp contrast to the green of the river bottom.

Early fur traders of French-Canadian stock called this stream the "Pelouse" or "Palouse,"[1] which might be translated rather freely as "the river with the green meadows." On the other hand, they might have been using a Nez Perce rather than a French-Canadian word, for the Nez Perce have a word, *peluse*, meaning "some-

thing sticking up out of the water."[2] This "something" is a ledge of rock, rising jaggedly above the rushing waters of the Snake just opposite the mouth of the Palouse River. It is the most dangerous spot in the whole reach of the notorious Texas Rapids, a menace to steamboats and barges for the last century.

Whatever the meaning of this river name, it is the forebear of *Appaloosa*, a modern word and the present-day name for the spotted horses in the United States and Canada. Although the spotted strain has been known to man for two hundred centuries or more, this name *Appaloosa* is less than a century old, and was coined during the 1870's. *Appaloosa* is an odd word. At first glance it might appear to come from one of the Indian dialects of the southeastern United States, possibly from Georgia. Attempts have been made to link *Appaloosa* through *Appaluchi* with *Appalachian*, or to derive it from *Apelousa*

---

[1] Alexander Ross, *Adventures of the First Settlers on the Oregon or Columbia River*, Vol. VII *Early Western Travels*, ed. Reuben Gold Thwaites, p. 208 n.

[2] Informant, Joseph Blackeagle, Nez Perce.

in the bayou country of Louisiana, but the word belongs to the Columbia Basin, coined by the men who handled the horses there, and is derived from the Palouse River which flows through that area.

When wheat farmers homesteaded the land along this stream in the 1870's the spelling for its name was fixed as *Palouse*, and in this form became official on the government maps. Local tradition recalls that at that time a Nez Perce living along the lower part of the stream owned a large herd of spotted horses. The wheat farmers soon were calling his horses "Palouse" or "Palousey horses," and this usage was applied to other spotted horses in the area. Then probably some newcomer who asked an old-timer the name of the strangely marked horses received the curt answer, "A Palousey." But the stranger, unfamiliar with the term, thought it all one word, and passed it along in writing as "an Apalousey," in which form it was known to the cowboys of Montana. Charlie Russell, the famous Montana cowboy painter, so wrote the word, and proved that he knew the kind of horse it was by putting the spotted animals in several of his pictures.

Through the ensuing years the spelling of the name has varied from place to place, but the form "Appaloosa" is now commonly accepted as the preferred version. Hence the club formed in 1938 to preserve the breed, and to promote public interest in this colorful horse of the Old West, chose *Appaloosa* as the spelling to be used.

Other Names for Spotted Horses

Since spotted horses have been known to man for twenty thousand years or more, and have been used for five thousand years in many different countries by people speaking many different languages, it is not surprising that such horses have been called by many different names. Yet the fact that some ancient people had a certain name for a type of riding horse does not necessarily mean that such a term was their name for spotted horses. Assurance that the name was applied to spotted horses usually requires the evidence of a picture or a statue of a spotted horse with the name attached. Here is a list of names which have been specifically applied to spotted horses in various countries:

Persia: *Kuran dagh*[3]
Austria: *Pinzgau*[4]
Denmark: *Knabstrupper, tigre*[5]
England: *Chubarry, Blagdon,*[6] *piebald*
Spain: *Chubarri, Atigrado*[7]
France: *Tigre*[8]
Argentina: *Tigre, pintado*[9]
Mexico: *Guinduri*[10] or *Wynduri*

[3] Letter (December 13, 1947) from Andrew Jeffery, Department of Semitic Languages, Columbia University, New York.
[4] Thornton Chard, "The Pinzgau Horse," *Western Horseman*, Vol. II, No. 5 (September–October, 1937), p. 11.
[5] Aksel Pederson, *Knabstruppere*, p. 1.
[6] Pedro A. Sarciat, *El Pelo Yaquane en el Caballo Criollo*, p. 60.
[7] *Ibid.*   [8] *Ibid.*   [9] *Ibid.*   [10] *Ibid.*

WATCHING FOR THE SMOKE SIGNAL. Charles M. Russell. The Amon Carter Museum of Western Art, Fort Worth, Texas.

Charles Russell arrived in Montana in 1880, less than four years after the disastrous defeat of Custer's men at the Big Horn, when feeling against the various tribes who opposed the spread of white settlers was still running high. From the first, however, Russell conceived a great sympathy for the Indians who defended their lands, and this sympathy was deepened by the time he lived among the Blood tribe of Canada as one of them. It shows quite clearly in all of his Indian paintings, even those that show them waging war. In this painting of a small band of warriors, Russell has painted not bloodthirsty savages, but men of courage and dignity. The Appaloosa in the center wears a "coup" mark on his shoulder, showing that he has already proven his worth to his master as a warhorse.

Rocky Mountains, 1830's: *Nez Perce horse*[11]
Mid-west: *Raindrop, dollar spot, leopard spot*[12]
China: probably *heavenly horse* or *blood-sweating horse*[13]
It is conjectured that the Sacred Horses of Nisaea, mentioned by Herodotus,[14] included some spotted stock. But in all these countries, under these names and many more, he remains the spotted horse.

Not all spotted horses, however, are Appaloosas. Certain well-defined characteristics mark the breed. The modern Appaloosa horse bred in the United States is most frequently identified by the unique markings on the rump. This frequently is seen as a "blanket" of white on which there may be spots or smaller flecks of one or more colors. Spots as a rule are round or egg-shaped and vary in size from mere specks to markings three or four inches in diameter. Some Appaloosas carry the spotting all over the body, but it is usually most dominant over the hips. Others show white over the hips without spots, and still others appear mottled all over the body or show white specks or spots with dark background.

Other important characteristics which must accompany the coat color and pattern are the white sclera encircling the eye and parti-colored skin especially noticeable about the nostrils. Significantly, while an Appaloosa may lose much of its color with age, the spots remain on the skin and may be readily seen under the hair. Hoofs are parti-colored, or striated vertically. An important factor in the Appaloosa's long-established reputation as a rough country traveler is the peculiar nature of the hoof, which provides the horse with protection against breaking on rocky ground.

General conformation is that of the close-coupled stock horse standing 14–2 to 15–2 hands high and weighing 950 to 1,100 pounds when mature.

Spotted Horses of the Ice Age

Fifty thousand years ago, as the last great ice sheet retreated slowly from Western Europe, a new breed of men came into central France. They were tall, long-headed Cromagnons, mighty hunters who followed the swarming herds of grazing animals to the new pastures uncovered by the retreating ice.

Near the great ice masses the winters were bleak and cold. Biting winds came howling down from the glacial mass at the north. Then the hunters sought such shelter as was offered by the deep, narrow valleys of central France, where westward-flowing streams had carved passageways through the high plateau. As these streams burrowed deeper and deeper into the rock formations of the Central Massif, they exposed great cliffs and ledges of limestone, honeycombed with shallow caves and deep caverns. In places the caverns extended miles into the mountains.

The shallow caves along the northern side of each val-

[11] William S. Lewis and Paul C. Phillips, *The Journal of John Work*, p. 110.
[12] Appaloosa Horse Club Archives, Moscow, Idaho.
[13] Pan Kuh, *The History of the Former Han Dynasty*, II, 102.
[14] *Herodotus*, Book VII, p. 40.

ley furnished shelter through the winter. The cliffs broke the sweep of the north wind while the low-hanging winter sun shone directly in to furnish warmth and comfort. In these shallow caves the Cromagnons built their cooking fires and roasted their meat over beds of coals. Here they dropped their well-gnawed bones to mix with the dirt and refuse of the floor. In time these bones, preserved from the weather by the overhanging rock, became covered with dirt. In modern times archeologists have dug into these refuse heaps, sorting and classifying the bones to find out what the Cromagnon family had for dinner in that far-off time. The bone piles show conclusively that over periods covering many centuries wild horses furnished much of the meat used by these people.

Just as the shallow caves furnished secure housing for these hunters, the deeper caverns supplied secret places for the mystic rites so necessary for the welfare of the tribe. Deep in the caverns the gifted men of the tribe worked their magic to insure to the grazing herds an ample crop of colts and calves each year. Other potent spells then brought the animals within reach of the hunter's weapons and made the kill certain.

For potent, effective magic, the magicians had to have lifelike paintings and statuettes of the kinds of animals they wished to control. The statuettes were molded in clay, or carved from bone or ivory. The smooth walls of the caverns furnished the surfaces for the paintings. Colored earths mixed with oil provided paints which have remained bright and clear for some two hundred centuries in these sheltered places. Hence some of these old paintings are almost as bright and clear as when they were new.

In time the walls and ceilings of the secret caverns were entirely covered with a profusion of animals. Then succeeding generations covered some of the original paintings with a second, and even a third, layer of new pictures. Here in the picture galleries of the Stone Age are found bison, reindeer, wild oxen, and wild horses, the same animals whose bones are found in large numbers in the refuse heaps.

The many paintings of the wild horses are of special interest to us, for they show plainly what the horses of Western Europe looked like in those days, with neat, clean heads, sharp-pointed ears, and trim legs. They also show that these animals, with their distended abdomens, are mares heavy with foal.

In two different caverns, separated by seventy miles of rough terrain, are horses with dark, symmetrical spots. In the cave at Lascaux, France, the basic color of the spotted horse is red or light brown. In the cave at Pêche-Merle the cave wall furnishes the body color, a light tan.

Although the kinds of horses pictured in these two caves display a marked similarity, it is not likely that one was copied from the other. Hence in those far-off times, in two separate hunting groups, spotted horses, important as food, were the objects of special rites and the sub-

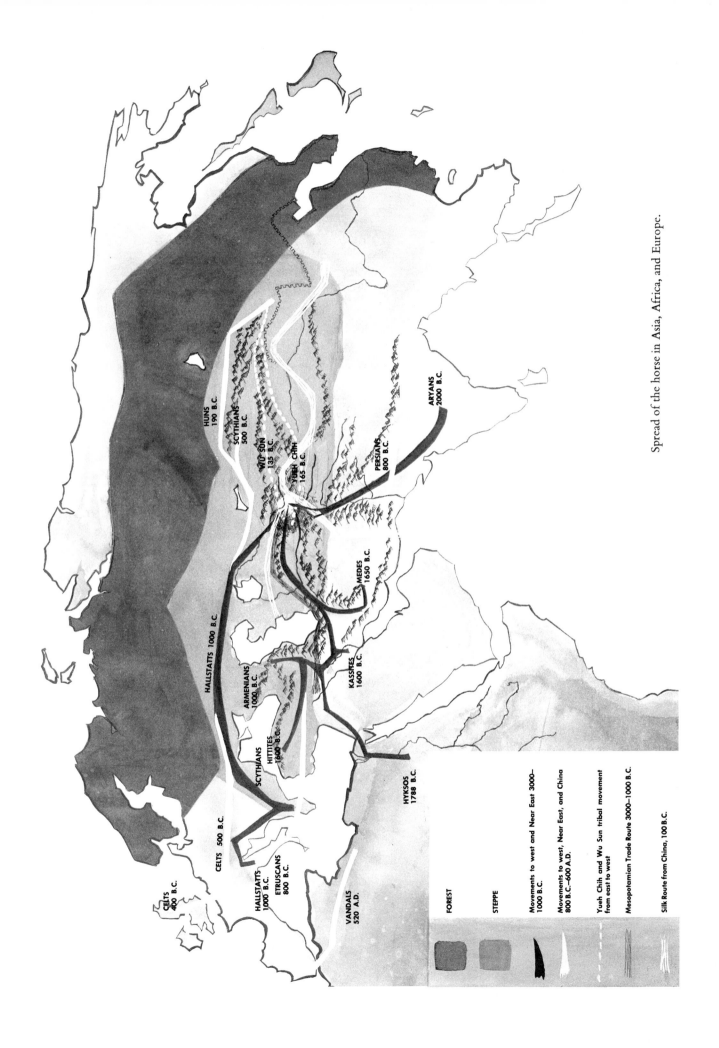

Spread of the horse in Asia, Africa, and Europe.

jects of mural art. These pictures, assigned to the Aurignacian culture, were drawn about 18,000 B.C.[15]

As represented in the pictures, these spotted horses were probably of the type which was the remote ancestor of the spotted horses of historic times. Sometime during the next twelve or thirteen thousand years man learned to tame this animal to be his servant as well as a source of food.

The First Horsemen

The years faded into centuries and the centuries rolled on. The ice sheet melted slowly, exposing broad plains which were soon covered with grass. Then the forests followed the grass in Western Europe until the trees reached the ocean shore. The grass eaters were crowded to the east, where fine pasture lands, the steppe country, stretched from western Russia to the highlands of southwestern Asia. The Paleolithic hunters followed the game, living along the edges of the steppes or in the parklands within the outer fringes of the forests.

These people became seminomadic, following the game in summer and retiring to small wattle-and-daub huts in the winter. They had the dog for a hunting companion. Then they learned to trap small herds of grass eaters in parks surrounded by natural barriers. The hunt-

ers could guard the one or two narrow entrances with watchmen and fires, and later with fences. In time they tamed some of the young animals and were able to raise their own meat supply. Here the first grazing animals to be tamed were the reindeer and the onager, domesticated about the same time, but probably by different villages. All this happened about 5000 B.C.[16]

A large group of long-headed Indo-Europeans then invaded the steppe country from the southeast. They are called the "Red Earth People," from their custom of coating their dead with red ochre. After this treatment the corpse was placed in a crypt, with a few horses and many other prized possessions for use in the spirit world. The burial place was then covered with a huge mound of earth, locally called a "kurgan."[17]

By this time the people of Mesopotamia had domesticated cattle, asses, goats, and sheep. They had developed the wheel and used it on carts and wagons, drawn by oxen, and had probably learned to ride both oxen and onagers.[18] The Red Earth People borrowed all this for their own use, probably through traders who came to the north shore of the Black Sea in ships. Then after several centuries they and their eastern neighbors took the

[15] Hans-Georg Bandi, Henri Breuil, *et al.*, *The Art of the Stone Age*, pp. 36–41, 53–55.

[16] James F. Downes, "The Origin and Spread of Riding in the Near East and Central Asia," *American Anthropologist*, LXIII (1961), 1193–1203.
[17] Harold Peake and Herbert John Fleure, *The Steppe and the Sown*, p. 20.
[18] Downes, *op. cit.*, p. 1193.

horse south to the valley folk, a story told in a later chapter.

The big event of the year for the Red Earth People was the midsummer religious festival. First they organized a long procession of horse-drawn carts and wagons loaded with offerings. When all the gifts reached the altar the horses were unhitched and sacrificed. Then followed a big feast for everyone. During this ceremony the carts and wagons were burned.

In time the horses came to be used as draft animals throughout the year. The carts were covered with light shelters, making small, portable sleeping quarters which were at least as warm and comfortable as the wattle-and-daub huts.[19] For many of the bands the next step was to become nomadic, traveling from place to place in search of game, and moving camp every day or so to insure plenty of grass for the animals and clean camp sites for the people. A camp of this kind becomes very messy over night, and it is much easier to move to a clean site than it is to clean up the garbage and refuse of the old one.

Certainly the problem of handling a horse herd in open grassland with teams for everyday use required at least a few mounted men for its solution. Since this fact is established by the experience of stockmen on the open ranges of the American West, it seems inevitable that some of the Red Earth People were competent riders.

[19] Peake and Fleure, *op. cit.*, p. 16.

Tribes on Horseback

Along the eastern edge of the steppes and in the small mountain valleys primitive men found food and shelter. Small garden patches in the alluvial soil along the streams produced vegetables and fruit for the scattered villages. Herds of grazing animals in the foothills and along the gently rolling grasslands furnished some meat and hides for the hunters who lay in wait for them along the game trails and near the watering places.

Walled in by the lofty snow-clad ranges on the east and the vast arid steppes on the west, the villagers were isolated from the rest of the world. Few of them cared to venture forth into the apparently endless plains to the west and northwest, their slow pace and puny weapons impotent against that immensity of space.

Then across the steppes from the west came small bands of men with their families and gear in horse-drawn carts.[20] The people of the foothills learned new skills and new ideas from the strangers. If these wanderers could use horses for servants, so could the villagers. Soon they were taming horses and breaking them to ride and drive.[21] Circumstances, however, made the hill people riders rather than drivers.

[20] Franz Hancar, *Das Pferd in Praehistorischer und Früher Historischer Zeit*, pp. 536–568. Hancar points out that there might have been at least two separate centers of domestication of horses, one in Russia, and one in the Asiatic steppes.
[21] *Cambridge Ancient History*, I, 25.

The carts were of less use in the foothills than on the steppes, and perhaps the horses raised in this higher pasture were stronger and tougher than those from the west. Certainly the smaller, lighter hill people, short-legged and wiry, made better riders than the larger-boned, fleshy men from the west. At any rate, the villagers became horsemen, and in time entire villages became nomadic, with their people and most of their possessions carried on horseback.

This type of horse culture spread north and east, where there was pasture for the herds, until it reached the farther bounds of Mongolia, making nomads of hundreds of thousands of people. Mounted on their swift steeds, the nomads found a new liberty, roaming the wide spaces on the wings of the wind. No longer were they bound to one small valley, forced to toil and sweat in their little garden patches for the bare necessities of life. Instead they became bold wayfarers, ranging to the limits of the steppes, with the vast ranges of the grasslands their home.[22]

In this new way of life the horse herd was the essential feature. The horses were riding animals, pack animals, animals to trade, and animals for meat. Milk from the mares became a major item of diet. In time of real need a rider could suck blood from a pierced vein of his mount and thus escape exhaustion and starvation. No wonder then that the nomads prized their horses above all else.

For some reason this area of Ferghana, between the

Oxus and Jaxartes rivers, produced superior horses, unsurpassed in size, strength, speed, intelligence, and endurance, and their fame spread in time from the shores of the Yellow Sea to the Mediterranean.[23] Around such horses legends cluster, myths are born, and the stories grow with the passing years. Kings and emperors prize them, artists immortalize them in bronze, marble, and jade. Poets sing of their charms, painters do their portraits. From these horse herds come special groups with the fanciful names, "The Heavenly Ones," "The Blood-sweating Breed," "The Sacred Horses," and the like.

For reasons not fully understood, wave after wave of horsemen from the steppes rode out south and west to conquer new lands. They all had close contact with the Ferghana area. Many of them do not belong in this story, but the list is imposing.

About 2000 B.C. Kassites and others entered Mesopotamia from the north. The invaders who pressed on to Egypt were the Hyksos, bringing the first horses to that land. By 1400 B.C. spotted horses appeared in Egyptian pictures.[24]

Another group, the Achaeans, went west and south into Greece. There, at Mycene in 1400 B.C., a spotted horse appeared on a vase.

The Hallstatt people moved west to Austria and on in

[22] Peake and Fleure, *op. cit.*, pp. 50–51.

[23] Tamara Talbot Rice, *The Scythians*, pp. 70–71.
[24] Walter A. Fairservis, Jr., *The Ancient Kingdoms of the Nile*, p. 124 n. mentions a horse skeleton of a time supposedly two hundred years earlier.

to northern Italy about 1000 B.C. At Hallstatt was found an iron sword scabbard dated about 800 B.C. and engraved with a row of four spotted horses.

In north Italy the Etruscans painted a spotted horse on a tomb wall about 800 B.C.

The Chinese emperor, Wu Ti, imported horses from Ferghana about 101 B.C. Soon spotted horses appeared in Chinese art.

The Persians claim that the ancestor of all spotted horses is the famous Rakush, Rustam's war horse.

These items considered together indicate that in the country of Ferghana and the pastures to the west there was a continuous supply of spotted horses in prehistoric and ancient times. These spotted animals were only a small portion of the total horse population of the area, probably a tenth or less, but because they appealed strongly to both the horsemen and the artists they received attention out of proportion to their numbers. The following pages recount the story of this interest in spotted horses.

In Ancient Egypt

IN ANCIENT TIMES the narrow, fertile valley of the Nile was well protected from invaders by the desert plateaus to the east and west. Here a civilization flourished for many centuries under the rule of a line of strong kings. Then the rulers grew weaker, and the whole land passed through a period of chaos. The weakened kingdom could not prevent the pastoral nomads from Palestine from crossing the desert and securing a foothold in the delta region.

At about the same time the horsemen from the Asiatic steppes began to invade Mesopotamia, conquering the valley folk by means of their horse-drawn war chariots. One band of invaders, the Hyksos, stormed out of Palestine about 1780 B.C. and crossed the desert wastes to Egypt, crushing all opposition under the wheels of their war chariots and the slashing hoofs of their spirited horses. The Egyptian foot soldiers fled in helpless terror before these strange, fierce animals. Then the Egyptians gradually assimilated the horses and chariots into their culture, and after a lapse of two or three centuries they overpowered the invaders.

Eventually Egyptian artists began using horses in tomb paintings and rock carvings, some of which survive today. These art objects have caused much discussion about the type of horse in ancient Egypt. Was that horse actually such a fragile creature, or were those slender limbs an artistic exaggeration? And just how large were those animals? Art critics realized that the Egyptian artists used a kind of "sliding scale" in fixing proportions among the various objects in their drawings: they selected for the central object in their paintings some royal or divine figure drawn on heroic scale to emphasize his importance; subordinate personages were drawn to a smaller scale; the slaves were still smaller in proportion. With animals, however, there is no known basis for de-

HORSES FROM PECHE-MERLE. Photograph by Carl Nesjar, Larvik, Norway. Courtesy of European Pictures, New York City.

Preliminary exploration of the cave at Pêche-Merle, situated west of the market town of Cabreret between the Lot and Garonne rivers in southwestern France, was undertaken in the early nineteen-twenties by the Abbé Lémozi, aided by a local archeologist, but the paintings also attracted the attention of the foremost authority on prehistoric art in France, the Abbé Breuil. Abbé Breuil assigns most of the paintings in this cave to the Aurignacian-Perigordian era at the beginning of the Upper Paleolithic. In the minds of the artists who painted these murals, their ritual significance probably dominated greatly their esthetic appeal. Caves where these paintings appear were never home sites. A connection with the theme of fertility of animals, on which the abundance of food for these early hunters depended, can be seen in the fact that both horses are pregnant mares. The silhouettes of hands which appear around the outlines of the horses also have some magical import. These handprints, together with rows and designs of dots in black and red, are a predominant motif in the paintings at Pêche-Merle.

termining relative importance, and so there is no way to tell what scale was used for horses, even when a human figure was shown near the animal. With only this evidence at hand, each historical scholar made his own estimate of the size of the horse in question. Most of them settled for a weak, spindly animal about fourteen hands or less in height. Now, in the light of new evidence, these estimates need to be revised.

In the course of Egyptian excavations archeologists have found the complete skeleton of a mummified horse of the New Kingdom Period. Here is a description of the skeleton:[1]

As now set up, the height of this skeleton, both at the withers and at the croup, is correct for a normal horse of medium weight, in relation to its length, and from a careful comparison of photographs of this skeleton with corresponding photographs of the skeleton of "Eclipse," the ancestor of most of the winning families of the English thoroughbred horses, it appears that this was the mummy of a somewhat powerfully built, moderately deep-chested, horse, with a strongly developed body frame and a large head.

This must have been an important horse in his day, to rate a mummy burial. Also the horses used as models for tomb paintings must have been of superior rank. Unless this mummified horse is an odd specimen among the Egyptian animals, it is evident that the Egyptian painters of the fourteenth century B.C. had a tendency to draw their horses a little slimmer in the chest and legs than they actually were. Statuettes of Egyptian horses of this period also indicate a stockier horse than those in the paintings.

The mummified horse and the statuettes indicate that some of the horses of Egypt in the period 1500–1300 B.C. were sturdy, well-shaped animals about fifteen hands in height and a thousand pounds in weight. They resemble in size and build the western stock horses of today.

Among the comparatively few representations of horses in Egyptian art of this period, two show horses with spots. One of these is from a tomb painting of 1415 B.C., the Tomb of Menena. This painting shows a chariot team of white horses with red spots. A glazed terra cotta statuette in the Oriental Institute Museum is a greenish horse with round brown spots. These two examples indicate that spotted horses were known to Egyptian artists during the period 1400–1300 B.C.[2]

An example of spotted horses in Egyptian textiles is the famous fabric fragment known as "the Quadriga Silk," now in the collection of the Patrimonie Artistique, Brussels, Belgium, which is attributed to a Syrian workshop in Alexandria, seventh-eighth century A.D.[3] By the fourteenth century the craftsmen in Syria were producing beautiful glassware ornamented with spotted horses.

---

[1] Alan Richard Schulman, "Egyptian Representations of Horsemen and Riding in the New Kingdom," *Journal of Near Eastern Studies*, XVI (January–October, 1957), 263, n. 4.

[2] *Ibid.*, p. 265, n. 20.
[3] *Das Textilwerk*, Introduction by Ernest Flemming, Plate 15.

VASE FROM MYCENAE. Courtesy of the National Museum, Athens, Greece.

When the warlike peoples who were to be known to history as the Greeks first came down to settle on the lands along the Aegean at the beginning of the second millennium B.C., they came into contact with the more peaceful and more civilized people of the Minoan culture centered on the island of Crete. The invaders established friendly relations with the older nation, and much inter-marriage took place between the two peoples. This vase fragment with a decoration of warriors in a chariot was found by the poros wall between the Tombs of Aegisthus and Clytemnestra outside the citadel at Mycenae. Possibly this vase, dating from the fourteenth century B.C., represents a scene from mythology, but it is too schematic to identify. The two-wheeled chariot may have been brought into Mycenae from Egypt, or it may have come from the lands around the Black Sea.

HARVEST SCENE. Photograph by the Egyptian Expedition of the Metropolitan Museum, 1927. Courtesy of the Metropolitan Museum of Art, New York City.

Perhaps this team of strikingly marked horses was a special favorite of Menena, an official of Pharaoh Thutmose IV, and were chosen for this reason to accompany him into the spirit world. With the scribes, overseers, and workers harvesting grain and fruit, they were painted on the wall of his tomb in the Necropolis of Thebes, *ca.* 1415 B.C., so that Menena might be as well served in his afterlife as he had been in Late Kingdom Egypt. Although the custom of filling tombs with paintings of three-dimensional models of the servants,

necessities, and luxuries that had surrounded their occupants in life was a part of the most ancient religious traditions of Egypt, the horse and two-wheeled chariot shown in this mural were comparatively new at this period. The two had come into the lands along the Nile with the Hyksos, a heterogeneous people from the steppes of Western Asia who overthrew the faltering rulers of Egypt around 1750 B.C. and shared the rule of Egypt with the pharaohs for a long period after the conquest. The horse-drawn vehicles used by the Hyksos troops had given them the margin necessary to conquer the older, richer nation, and the Egyptians learned, the hardest way possible, to value the horse as an element of warfare.

Horses in Northwestern Africa

A horse was a rarity to the Egyptians before the invasion of the Hyksos in 1780 B.C. Early Egyptian expeditions to the west found no trace of such animals in the pastures of Libya. About 2475 B.C. King Sahure of Egypt, in an extensive raid to the west, captured large herds of cattle, asses, goats, and sheep, but the detailed account of this expedition makes no mention of horses. A similar raid by Ramses III after the arrival of the Hyksos, about 1175 B.C., found horses in abundance in the same area.[4]

It is probable that the people of Libya could have secured some horses from Egypt as early as 1700 B.C., although there is no positive evidence to support this. There is valid evidence showing that sea-faring people from Crete and Asia Minor crossed in their ships to Libya about 1400 B.C. and brought horses and chariots with them.[5]

In those days the climate of northern Africa was moister, and Libya had excellent pasture lands. As the horses increased rapidly in this favorable environment, the nomadic horsemen spread rapidly to the south and west. Hundreds of their rock paintings still preserved in the Sahara show clearly their horses and horse gear, but never do they show a horse with spots.

As the centuries sped by, these nomads joined in the great wars, sometimes fighting against the city state of Carthage, sometimes joining with Carthage against Rome, but in the end Rome conquered and occupied all the farm lands along the northern African coast. Carthage was burned to the ground and the ruins were sown with salt, but a new Carthage rose from the ashes as a Roman city, only to be conquered by the Vandals who had crossed at the Straits of Gibraltar and had moved east along the coast.

During the period of Vandal domination of the coast, a wealthy landowner built himself a fine country villa, adorned on the walls and floors with mosaic pictures showing scenes about the estate. Two of these mosaics contain spotted horses of about life size, indicating that such horses were used on the estate about 520 A.D.

Up to the present time (1962) this is the only positive evidence of spotted horses in northern Africa between the border of Egypt and the Atlantic. So far, attempts to find spotted horses, or records of spotted horses, in this area have been in vain.

Even the French cavalry remount service has failed to find such horses. The French held Algeria from 1831 to 1962, and exercised a protectorate of sorts over Morocco during most of the nineteenth century. To combat the nomadic tribes to the south the French army made extensive use of cavalry, and bought many horses locally each year to supplement those imported from France. Hence the French had definite information on horse breeders and horse types in Morocco, Algeria, and Tunis —but they found no spotted horses.

In 1947 the American consul general at Casablanca,

[4] J. K. Anderson, *Ancient Greek Horsemanship*, p. 32.
[5] Henri Lhote, *The Search for the Tassili Frescoes*, pp. 125 ff.

MOSAIC FROM CARTHAGE. Courtesy of the Trustees of the British Museum, London.

Carthage, the city which, according to Roman legend, was founded by the Phoenician Queen Dido, probably began as a trading settlement for Phoenician traders and seamen crossing the Mediterranean to obtain metal ores from the mines of Spain and Cornwall. It was one of the chief cities in North Africa during the Roman Empire, and under Roman rule the province was a bread-basket for Rome's teeming populace. Roman control was destroyed by the Vandal invasions from Spain in the fifth century A.D., and the city became little more than a pirates' nest. Some of the Vandal rulers maintained the public buildings and basilicas built by their Roman predecessors, or built new ones in traditional Roman style. This mosaic of a rider on a spotted horse, part of the decoration of a villa near Carthage made about 520 A.D., shows that some of the minor arts inherited from Rome were also continued. This type of horse may have come with the Vandals, for the entire area of North Africa has yielded few examples of spotted horses in art or in history.

Morocco, made extensive inquiries among the horse experts there. They all agreed that Morocco possessed none of the spotted horses of the Appaloosa type, except as very rare freaks, which were quickly bought up by the circuses.[6]

This material on Libya and Morocco has been emphasized to show that as yet no evidence exists to support either the "Libyan Leopard" or the "Moroccan Barb." Both of these seem to be inventions of Americans with fertile imaginations—and with little knowledge of the subject.

The Sacred Horses of Nisaea

About 2000 B.C. powerful tribes of Indo-Europeans moved south from the steppes and took over the Iranian Plateau. They borrowed from the Babylonians the new-type war chariot with the light, strong-spoked wheel. Soon they had mastered its use, and their forces moved out along four invasion paths. One prong crossed the mountains to the southeast and invaded India, where they are known as Aryans. A second group, the Kassites, took over Babylonia. The third prong split, with the Mittani conquering Armenia and the Hittites the interior of Asia Minor. The fourth prong swung to the north of the Black Sea and moved south into the Greek peninsula. These people Homer called the Achaeans.

The Mittani developed chariot horses and a careful method of conditioning them for warfare; they ruled for several hundred years before bowing to the Assyrians. These tough fighting men from Arabia, who held a small area in the hills between the Tigris and Euphrates rivers for centuries before they moved out as conquerors, rose to power about 910 B.C. and dominated the Near East for three hundred years.

The Assyrians combined the use of the war chariot with bands of armed horsemen, using the same type of horse for both riding and driving. Surviving sculptures from Assyrian palaces show these horses with neat heads, trim legs, and sturdy bodies, closely resembling the western stock horse of today.[7] The Assyrians secured their best horses from the Medes north across the mountains on the Iranian Plateau. By this time the Medes were noted for their fine horses, raised on pastures of alfalfa.

The Assyrians prized white horses above all others, reserving them for temple sacrifices. The Assyrian ruler, Ashur-bani-apal, was deeply impressed by three white horses sent by the king of Elam, indicating that such horses were scarce in the Tigris-Euphrates valley.[8]

Finally the Assyrians gave way to new invaders from the north. In 612 B.C. the Medes and Persians, with their

[6] Letters from Charles W. Lewis, Jr., U.S. Consul General, Casablanca, Morocco, May 8, 1947; and Colonel Le Vavasseur, French Army, Casablanca, Morocco, May 8, 1947.

[7] R. D. Barnett, *Assyrian Palace Reliefs*, Panels 14, 15, 18, 20, 21, and 24.

[8] A. T. Olmstead, *History of Assyria*, p. 460 (p. 75 in 1956 edition).

superior cavalry and a surging vitality, took over from the war-weary Assyrians. They captured the lands and the horses. The Persians sacrificed horses in the temples, but they also used many for meat. Each day several were slaughtered with the rest of the meat animals at the king's palace. At the yearly festival for the god Mithras, twenty thousand plump foals were sacrificed and roasted to feed the vast crowd of worshippers.[9]

Persian carvings of horses show animals much heavier and more blocky than the trim Assyrian horse.[10] The coarser bone structure is shown particularly in the head and the legs. The Persian horse has also a pronounced Roman nose. From their appearance, the horses of the carvings could be special stock fattened for slaughter.

It is obvious that the Persians had brought in a new, heavier strain of horse, and may have crossed it with the smaller horses of earlier times. However, it is unlikely that horses as bulky as these sacrificial animals were used either in the cavalry or with the war chariots. Hence the Persians probably had two kinds of horses, the bulky, heavy type for meat and sacrifices, and the Assyrian type for use in war.

The twenty thousand foals for the feast of Mithras and the horses for the king's table were raised in Media, where the king kept a royal herd of fifty thousand animals. Some of them were pure white, and were especially prized. They hauled the sacred chariot of Ormazd in the state processions, or were led along, decked in elaborate trappings. It has been suggested that only these special white horses should carry the name, "the Sacred Horses of Nisaea," but it is obvious that both Herodotus,[11] the Greek historian, and Strabo,[12] the Greek geographer, used this name for the entire herd, and for some of the war horses.

So far no representation of the Nisaean horse which plainly shows that some of these animals were spotted has been found, but there are bits of evidence pointing to this conclusion. In Greek art at about the time of the Persian invasion appear a few representations of spotted animals which could have been inspired by the horses of King Xerxes. Some scholars link the Sacred Horses of Nisaea with the Heavenly Horses of Wu Ti, through the horses of Ferghana, and it is probable that some of the horses of Wu Ti were spotted.[13] In addition, Persian legend holds that the first spotted horse was Rakush, the original sire of the superior Persian horses. In the Persian legend Rakush was sired by a white demon of the mountains, which in Persian folklore is a friendly spirit. The Chinese version is that the superior horses were sired by a dragon, again a friendly spirit.

The Persian Empire had a stormy history, and finally succumbed to Alexander of Macedon, whose successors

[9] A. T. Olmstead, *History of the Persian Empire*, p. 291.
[10] Anderson, *op. cit.*, Plates 8, 39.

[11] Herodotus, *op. cit.*, Book IX, Sec. 21, Vol. II, p. 639.
[12] Strabo, *Geography*, translated by H. C. Hamilton and W. Falconer, II, 7, 13.
[13] Arthur Waley, "The Heavenly Horses of Fergana," *History Today*, V (February, 1955), pp. 95–103.

gave way in turn to a new body of horsemen from the north, the Parthians. These people developed a heavy cavalry, with both men and horses protected by leather armor covered with overlapping metal rings. Some historians argue that the Parthians needed large, heavy horses to carry the weight of the man and the armor,[14] but the few pictures extant do not show such a large horse.

A good western stock horse of the present day is able to carry a total load of 250 pounds. This horse weighs from 1,000 to 1,100 pounds, and the load consists of a 200-pound rider with an allowance of 50 pounds for saddle and gear. The Parthians were much smaller men, and used lighter saddles. He could allow 80 to 100 pounds for armor for himself and his horse, and not go over the 250-pound total. Hence the "great Parthian war horse" need not have been so large after all. This point is important in the history of the Heavenly Horses of Wu Ti.

The Heavenly Horses of Wu Ti

Once the tribesmen of the steppes learned the art of horsemanship, the bands of horsemen multiplied rapidly. They occupied all of Mongolia and Manchuria where pastures could be found. In the course of time their raiding and plundering became a serious threat to the Chinese farming villages and towns to the south and east, from which they would vanish before the Chinese soldiers could punish them.

Developments from this situation along the Chinese border during the second century B.C. were significantly related to the history of the spotted horse. For centuries the great foe of China from the north was the Hsiung Nu, the Huns of European history. As their numbers increased and their cavalry tactics improved, the Huns threatened to wipe out the entire farming population in the northern provinces. To protect the exposed frontier the Chinese built a great wall from the coast of the Yellow Sea to the mountains some fourteen hundred miles inland. As long as the Great Wall was kept in repair and was supplied with an adequate garrison, the raiding Huns were held in check. Stalled in their drive to the south, the nomads turned westward, driving out smaller tribes and occupying the foothills of the Tien Shan range.[15]

A succession of weak emperors to the throne of China brought on a period of internal confusion and a weakening of the northern defenses. Finally, in 144 B.C., Wu Ti, greatest of the Han Dynasty, secured the crown. He soon repaired the Great Wall and sent his cavalry patrols to the north of it. They were to harry the Huns in their own lands and to give warnings of any mass attacks. These tactics kept the Huns at bay, but at a high cost. Each year thousands of recruits and tens of thousands of new horses were needed to keep the border armies at full

---

[14] W. W. Tarn, *The Greeks in Bactria and India*, p. 308, n. 4.

[15] *Ibid.*, pp. 276–277.

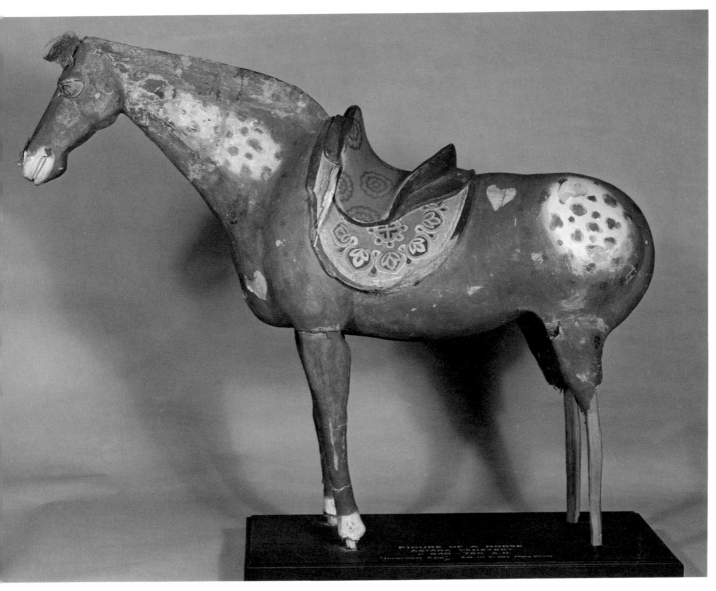

TOMB HORSE. In the Collection of The British Museum. Photograph from *On Central Asian Tracks*, by Sir Aurel Stein. Courtesy of the Trustees of the British Museum, London.

This statuette of a horse was excavated from a tomb of T'ang Dynasty date at Astana, Turfan, by Sir Aurel Stein, in the eastern part of Sinkiang Province, China. It is similar to the much finer ceramic horses, often decorated in three-colored glazes found in tombs in China at this period. In China figurines of horses are found in tombs of the Han Dynasty (206 B.C. to 221 A.D.). They were substituted for real horses, which it had been customary to bury with their masters since the Shang originated the practice during the second millennium B.C. This horse probably dates around the seventh century A.D. It is one of the earliest representations of horses marked with the light hips and spots of the Appaloosa to be found in Asia. Not far from the site of these tombs, in the caves of Tun-huang, a large number of spotted horses appear in a magnificent series of murals. Many of these murals have been assigned a similar T'ang date and are contemporary with the statuette illustrated.

strength. It is a matter of official record that the Chinese armies lost 100,000 horses in the campaigns of the year 119 B.C.[16]

At that time the Chinese horses were small, ewe-necked, and pot-bellied. Although fairly sturdy, they were slow of foot and rather small for effective cavalry mounts. Their greatest defect, however, was that their hoofs were too soft to withstand long marches in rocky or desert country. The Chinese fashioned them shoes of leather or braided straw, but these were both costly and ineffective. This failure of the horses' hoofs accounted in a large measure for the excessive horse casualties on campaigns, and the army's need each year for a large number of new horses.

The Huns intensified the problem by raiding the imperial pastures at every opportunity. These pastures, thirty-six in number, held from eight thousand to ten thousand horses each, and supplied some fifty thousand horses to the army each year, if the Huns did not raid them first. In addition, the farmers were encouraged to raise horses, which brought high, fixed prices. Even so the army was often short of horses and had to postpone planned operations. Understandably, Emperor Wu Ti was interested in securing better horses.

Court officials sought superior horses as presents for the Emperor, knowing this was a sure road to favor. One official, Pao Li Chang, had been exiled to a garrison on

EIGHT HORSES. Attributed to Chao Meng-fu. Detail from left end of scroll. Courtesy of the Metropolitan Museum, New York, Kennedy Fund, 1913.

While Chao Meng-fu (1254–1322 A.D.) is known to Occidentals chiefly for his paintings of horses, in China he is equally famous as a calligrapher and statesman. Chao lived during the Yüan Dynasty (1279–1368 A.D.), when China was ruled by the Mongols, and he served as an official at the court of Kublai Khan. According to tradition, Chao modeled his horse paintings after those of Han Kan of the T'ang Dynasty.

[16] Pan Kuh, *op. cit.*, p. 66, n. 16. 7.

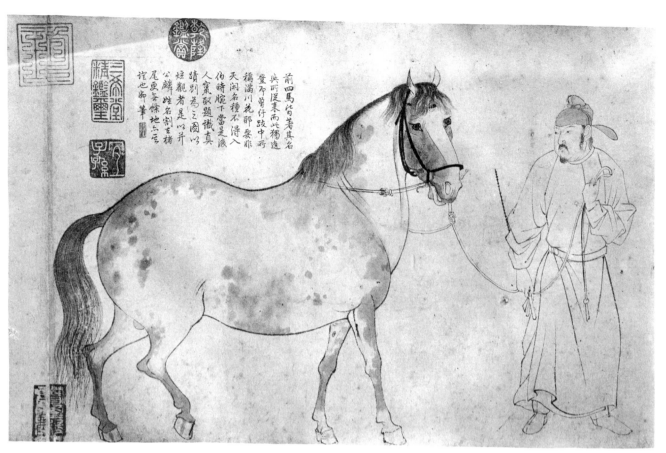

前四馬皆著其名
興所提未而此獨逸
登所曾行跋中所
稱滿川花郎要非
天閑名種不浸入
公時院下當是後
人竊取題識真
蹟別為之圖以
矬粗者是以井
尾更吾餘地太守
詫也師筆

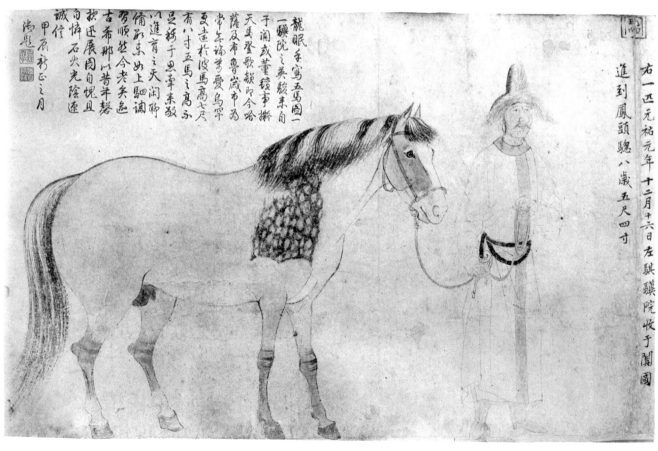

龍眠手寫五馬圖一
一驥院之英骏来自
于闐戓董鎮事摟
天馬登歌韻今哈
薩及布魯歲市為
常年諭等愛烏罕
夏畫枏浚馬高七尺
有八寸五馬之高亦
足矯于里牽末來敬
八進育之天閑師
備郫東如上馳调
寫順並今老矣遠
古希那以昔年聲
向怛展圄自愧且
誠作石火光陰速
甲辰新正之月
滿题

右一匹元祐元年
十二月十六日左驍騏
院收于閩國
進到鳳頭驄八歲五尺四寸

WESTERN HORSES AND THEIR GROOMS. Photographs courtesy of the Fine Arts Library, the University of Michigan, Ann Arbor.

Li Lung-mien was a member of the circle of poets, artists, and philosophers who flourished during the Sung Dynasty, one of China's golden eras. He shares with Kan Kuan, of the earlier T'ang Dynasty, the reputation as the most renowned of the many famous painters of horses in the history of Chinese art. These horses, painted about 1086–1087 A.D., represent tribute horses sent to the Chinese emperor from Khotan and other western countries. Executed in a monochrome style called "nakubyo-twa," this scroll gives what seems to be individual portraits of both horses and grooms. The horses stand at ease or walk slowly, moving with all the dignity expected of animals soon to join the imperial stables. Of the five, three show spotting in their coats. The scroll has a text written by a contemporary poet, Huang Shan-ku, a practice common in the Sung Dynasty, when poets would compose verses for artists' paintings and the artists reciprocated with illustrations for poems. This scroll, apparently the only work of this artist which survived into the twentieth century, was formerly part of the Imperial Manchu Household Collection. Later it was in the Kikkuli Collection in Tokyo and is believed to have been destroyed in World War II.

the northwestern frontier for some trivial mistake. Here he noticed a horse of unusual beauty in a wild herd that came each day to drink at the river. According to the old story, Pao Li Chang made a clay figure of a man holding a halter and hobbles. This he placed on the river bank near the watering place. After the wild horses had become accustomed to the clay figure, he took its place and managed to capture the wild stallion, so different from the others, and sent it to the emperor. Since Pao Li Chang wanted special appreciation for his present, he stretched the story a little, claiming that this was a supernatural horse which had come to him out of the river mist.[17]

Emperor Wu Ti, in his search for allies against the Huns, planned to enlist the Yueh Chih in a joint attack on the common enemy. These fierce and determined warriors, among the chief opponents of the Huns on their westward march, had retreated before superior numbers to Ferghana, a frontier province of Persia. Emperor Wu Ti sent a courageous, resourceful court official, Chang Ch'ien,[18] to the west in 138 B.C. to find the Yueh Chih in their new location. While on this search Chang was captured by the Huns and was held as an honored prisoner for ten years, until he escaped.

A few years later, in 115 B.C., Chang Ch'ien was sent again as envoy, this time to the Wu-Sun. From this mis-sion he brought back a number of the horses from the west, which were so superior to the Chinese horses that they were thought to be the horses prophesied in the Book of Changes, which said "the heavenly horse will come from the North West."

After Chang Ch'ien's death in 114 B.C. the Emperor heard news of another "heavenly horse" in Ferghana, which was supposed to be much superior to the horses of the Wu-Sun. It is probable that these were some of the sacred horses reserved for temple sacrifice, and Emperor Wu Ti was deeply interested in any sort of sacrifice or religious rite which might speed him to heaven when he died.[19] This superstitious interest of the Emperor helps account for his sustained efforts over the next few years to secure some of these special horses.

First the Emperor sent an embassy with rich gifts and a supply of gold. Various accounts are given of the details of this venture, but they all agree that the envoy was killed. Then the Emperor ordered out his army under his best general, Li Kuang Li. Two thousand miles of arid country hindered the march. The army had to capture each water hole along the way, and ran short of food when the transport failed. The shattered and disgraced remnants reached the border of their homeland only to find the Jade Gate closed against them.

Here they camped for weary months while the Emperor's officials back home scoured the country for more

[17] *Ibid.*, II, 75, n. 19. 6.
[18] Burton Watson, *Records of the Grand Historian of China.* This work contains the report of Chang Ch'ien.

[19] Waley, *loc. cit.*

THE ONE HUNDRED COLTS. Reproduced from *Chinese Pictorial Art*, by Herbert A. Giles.

Though his reputation depends mainly upon references in Chinese literature, Han Kan is considered to have been one of China's greatest horse painters. As a painter at the court of the T'ang emperor Hsuan-tsung (reigned 713–756 A.D.), Han Kan could not have wanted for subject matter; the Emperor is said to have had more than forty thousand horses in his stables. Many of these horses were sent to the Emperor as tributes from Ferghana and other western countries. No unquestionably identified work of Han Kan survives today, but works by later artists said to be copies after the great T'ang painter are extant. This sixteenth-century woodcut roundel is supposed to be based on a design by Han Kan.

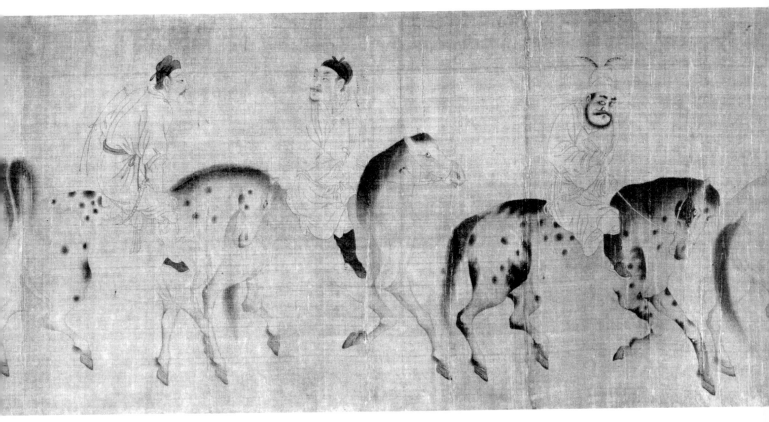

EIGHT HORSES AND THEIR TARTAR RIDERS. Detail of Scroll. Courtesy of the Museum of Fine Arts, Boston, Massachusetts.

The horses and their Tartar riders trot briskly across the surface of the silk. The animated, almost grotesque features of the Tartars is a typical formula used by Chinese artists in depicting foreigners. The absence of background details to detract from the riders and their horses focuses attention upon the Tartars' remarkable ability to ride bareback.

A HALT FOR REST. Chao Yung. Courtesy of the Metropolitan Museum, New York, Kennedy Fund, 1913.

Chao Yung, the son of Chao Meng-fu, is also famous for his horse paintings. Growing up in an artistic household—his mother, Kuan Tao-sheng, and an uncle, Chao Meng-yu, were both well-known painters—it is not surprising that Chao Yung continued the family tradition. His style in painting appears to have been strongly influenced by that of his father.

men, horses, and supplies. All archers in the prisons of China were drafted, along with all the young men with bad reputations. By various means an army of sixty thousand was raised. One hundred thousand oxen, thirty thousand horses, and tens of thousands of donkeys, mules, and camels carried the supplies. Two of the best judges of horses in China were sent along to select the best from any captured herds.

This time General Li was successful. He reached the capital and placed it under siege. The local ruler sent a call for help to the neighboring nomads, but the nobles, possibly Macedonian officials, preferred surrendering to the civilized Chinese rather than admitting such dubious allies to their city. They made an agreement with General Li that they would kill their ruler and would make peace at once if the Chinese would agree to keep their troops outside the city. In addition, General Li could have some horses.[20]

The Chinese selected about twenty-five of the very special horses, and about three thousand of the others. It is probable that these compared favorably with the choice horses from the Wu-Sun, since the Wu-Sun were close neighbors. While there is no detailed description of these animals, their appearance was soon evident in Chinese art.[21]

From the sculptures, these horses appear to have been of the western stock horse type, sturdy, close-coupled animals. They had greater endurance than the earlier Chinese type, and their hoofs were tougher. Of special importance in relation to the Appaloosa is a group of these horses represented on a tomb tile. On the hips of these animals is a spiral marking which one scholar states was an artistic convention to indicate the markings of a horse.[22] This would indicate that some of the horses from the west were of the spotted breed.

The Chinese had friendly relations with the Wu-Sun for many years after Chang Ch'ien's first visit. To cement the friendship, the Chinese envoys offered a Chinese princess, Hsi Chün, as a bride for the chief of the Wu-Sun. A thousand of the western horses went to the Emperor as a betrothal gift, and in due course the princess arrived to marry K'un-mo.

From the time of the Emperor Wu Ti, the Chinese had a steady flow of horses from the west. They also located most of their stock farms west of the Yellow River. The records of the importation of horses are far from complete, but occasionally actual figures are given: For the year 611 A.D. is the entry that a Turk came from the west with a thousand horses to trade; the next year he appeared with two thousand horses, but some of these were for his own use; a few months later the Chinese

---

[20] Pan Kuh, *op. cit.*, II, 132.
[21] Letter to the author from Thomas Lawton, Cambridge, Massachusetts, July 26, 1962.

[22] Charles William White, *Tomb Tile Pictures of Ancient China*, pp. 40–43.

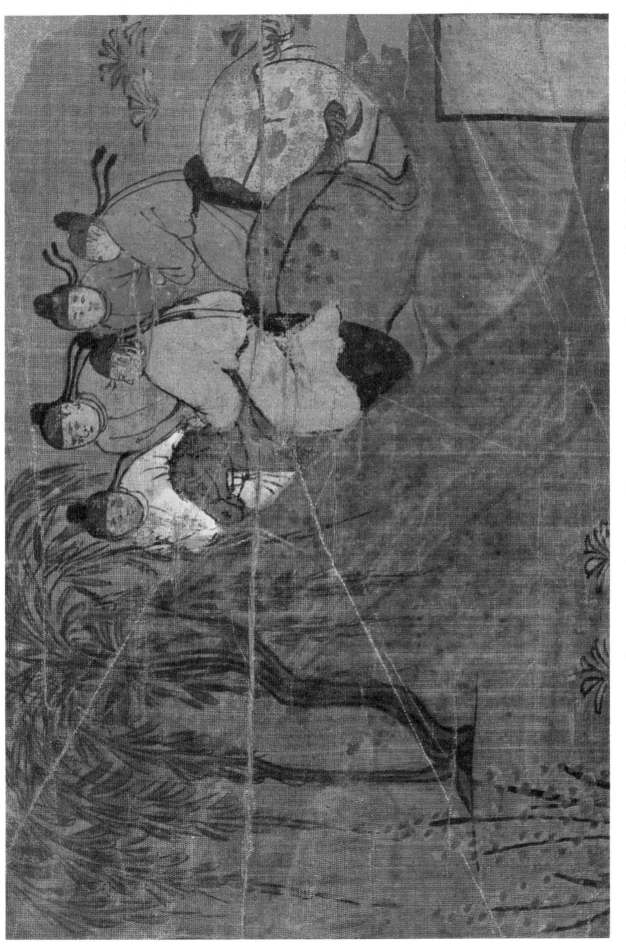

SEARCHING FOR THE BUDDHA. The Stein Collection. Courtesy of the Trustees of the British Museum, London.

The Caves of the Thousand Buddhas, located near the Tun-huang oasis in Kansu Province, provide an invaluable source for early examples of Chinese painting. Most of the paintings from Tun-huang illustrate events found in Buddhist texts. This silk fragment in the British Museum represents a group of five men searching for Prince Siddharta after he had secretly left the palace to meditate in the wilderness. Details, such as the flowers and trees, give some indication of the Chinese artists' increasing concern with organizing the elements of nature into a coherent landscape.

bought horses and hired some mounted warriors from the west in exchange for silk and treasure.[23]

By using many of the western horses for breeding, and by importing new stock, the Chinese eventually had enough of the better horses for use with the crack cavalry units. As a result the range and effectiveness of the cavalry were increased. This in turn stimulated the military experts to devise new tactics and weapons for utilizing the potential of the horses. A new light crossbow, which could be used by a mounted man, enabled the Chinese cavalry to outrange the Hun archers, and to push them back from the northern frontier.

For centuries the Chinese held their advantage, losing battles only when the troops were poorly led or inadequately trained. During this same period the Huns moved to the west and invaded Europe. It is possible, then, that the introduction of superior horses from the west into China was indirectly responsible for the attacks of Attila in Europe in the fifth century A.D.

Chinese art provides interesting revelations concerning horses in China. T'ai Tsung, first of the T'ang Dynasty, fought his way to the throne of China in a series of campaigns from 611 to 613 A.D. Under the T'angs, Chinese art experienced a great growth. New methods and techniques were developed. Ceramic plates and statuettes were coated with fine glaze in two and three colors.

Large numbers of the statuettes were made for burial with the dead, and were preserved in the burial mounds until the present time. The numerous statuettes representing horses show two distinct types. Less common but more dramatic is the great war horse, complete with trappings, often shown with ears laid back, mouth open, and one forefoot pawing the air. The more common type is much like the modern stock horse, well-knit, close-coupled, and about fifteen hands high. Both types are shown with spots.

When T'ai Tsung died in 637 his tomb was decorated with bas-relief statues of his six famous war horses, each honored with a poem commemorating the battle in which he had carried the Emperor to victory. One of the six, Ching Chui, was Blue Piebald, a spotted horse. Here is his poem:

> Lightfooted streak of lightning
> It was high spirited
> I whipped up this flying steed
> And was able to lay down my armor.[24]

From the seventh century A.D. the spotted horse is common in Chinese art down to the present day. Since there is no record of the introduction of any new type of horse into China from the time of Wu Ti and the reign of T'ai Tsung, it is probable that the first spotted horses

[23] Woodbridge Bingham, *The Founding of the T'ang Dynasty*, pp. 95, 99, 123.

[24] John C. Ferguson, "The Six Horses at the Tomb of the Emperor T'ai Tsung of the T'ang Dynasty," *Eastern Art*, III (1931), 61–71.

HUNTING SCENE IN LANDSCAPE. Detail of Scroll. Courtesy of the Museum of Fine Arts, Boston, Massachusetts.

The dynamic use of the long handscroll was especially popular during the Ming Dynasty (1368–1644 A.D.). By varying the tempo throughout the scroll, the Ming artist has captured something of the growing excitement of the hunt. At the beginning of the scroll, the emperor sits quietly astride his horse as two attendants sound the drum and bell. As the scene unfolds, the hunters gradually increase their speed until they are galloping through the colorful landscape. This detail shows a huntsman astride his spotted mount at the moment of peak excitement, closing in for the kill.

MEN GROOMING HORSES UNDER TREES. Detail of Scroll. Ross Collection. Courtesy of the Museum of Fine Arts, Boston, Massachusetts.

The Mongols, who ruled China during the Yüan Dynasty (1279–1368 A.D.), were fond of riding and hunting. Their love of horses no doubt prompted them to encourage the artists of the period to paint scenes in which horses played an important role. The degree of excellence attained by the painters of horses in this period was acknowledged by the artists of the succeeding dynasty, who used earlier works as models rather than attempting original treatments of the subject. Though executed during the Ming Dynasty (1368–1644 A.D.) this painting representing a group of horses being cared for by their grooms is traditionally said to have been based on such a Yüan prototype.

came in from the west with the horses from the Wu-Sun and from Ferghana in the period 112–101 B.C.

Spotted horses were common in China for at least the last thirteen hundred years, and probably for two thousand years, but they never composed more than a small fraction of the horses of the country. There is no accurate estimate of the ratio of spotted horses to others, but it seems improbable that this could have been greater than one in ten, even in the selected stock.

It is reasonable to conjecture that the special horses of Ferghana were those set apart for the temple sacrifices, and so were possibly of the sacred breed of Nisaea. The "several tens" of these special horses brought to China in 101 B.C. were known at the court of Emperor Wu Ti as "Heavenly Horses," but there is no indication that the three thousand horses of lesser quality were included in this class. It is indicated that these Heavenly Horses were the kind sacrificed at the funeral of the Emperor.[25]

[25] "It was avowedly in reprisal for this action (though Waley suggests this was just a pretext which allowed the Emperor to fulfill his own quest for immortality) that General Li Kuang-li (brother of the emperor's favorite concubine) undertook his two expeditions of 104 and 102 B.C. When he returned to China in 101 B.C., it turned out that the Ferghana horses were indeed much finer than those of the Wu-sun. Consequently the name 'Heavenly Horse' was given to the Ferghana type, while the Wu-sun horses were called 'Horses from the Western Extremity.' Though Li Kuang-li selected several tens of the best Ferghana horses, and more than 300 ordinary stallions, and mares, he returned with only 1000 horses. The rest succumbed to the rigors of the trek back to China." Letter from Thomas Lawton, Cambridge, Massachusetts, July 26, 1962. Lawton bases this summary on several sources of both Occidental and Oriental scholars.

By the seventh century A.D. the sacrificial horses were represented in the burial ceremonials in western China by statuettes,[26] rather than by the actual animals. Since many of these statuettes are of spotted horses, it is probable that some of the original Heavenly Horses of Wu Ti were spotted.

A common descriptive term for the western horses was "blood sweating." Scholars have two explanations for the use of this term. One is that the Chinese borrowed from some foreign language an expression which sounded like the Chinese phrase, "blood sweating," and in the course of time the origin of the word and its early meaning have been lost.

A Chinese poet links the term with the Heavenly Horse:

> A gift from the Supreme One
> The heavenly horses have been sent down.
> They are dampened by a sweat;
> Their foam flows blood.[27]

The second explanation is derived from a tradition and a fact related to spotted horses. To this day the horses of central Asia are reported to be infested with a parasite which produces swellings under the skin along the shoulders and the backs of the horses. When these horses are exercised, the swellings bleed a little, forming small spots of blood-clotted hair around the openings. From a short distance these spots resemble the natural

[26] Aurel Stein, *Innermost Asia*, IV, Plate XCIX.
[27] Pan Kuh, *op. cit.*, II, 133.

MEN AND HORSES UNDER TREES. Style of Chao Meng-fu. Detail of Scroll. Courtesy of the Museum of Fine Arts, Boston, Massachusetts.
  Like so many Ming paintings depicting horses and their grooms, the hanging scroll from which this detail (a groom riding a spotted horse into a river to water the animal) was taken is said to have been painted in the style of Chao Meng-fu. Later generations of artists honored the great horse painter of the Yüan Dynasty by imitating his style of painting to such an extent that their work can be identified by this style alone, even though they are anonymous. Surrounded by an idyllic landscape and guarded by their grooms, the horses graze quietly. The precise, rather tight brushstrokes and the opaque colors are typical of the period.

JAPANESE INRO, silver. Courtesy of the Museum of Fine Arts, Boston, Massachusetts.

Inrō are medicine cases or pill boxes. This seventeenth-century example is made in five sections, providing the owner with separate containers for various medicines. The spotted charger, snorting to show his spirit and mettle, is executed in multicolor lacquer and the design curves almost completely around the circular container. Actually *inrō* were used mainly as ornaments. Fashionable Japanese gentlemen wore them at their waists to enhance their appearance.

spotting of the horses shown in the Chinese pictures, and the term "blood sweating" might have been applied to all the spotted horses whether the horses actually sweated blood or not. This would be a usage similar to the term "flea-bitten" now applied to horses with very small spots on gray or white basic color.

Gradually the Chinese allowed their horses to deteriorate. European visitors in the nineteenth century found the average horse more like those of long ago—small, coarse, and poorly kept. Paintings of this period still show some good stock, with a spotted horse here and there, and spotted horses were raced at Shanghai as late as 1931.[28]

[28] Appaloosa Horse Club Archives, Moscow, Idaho.

Spotted Horses in Korea, Japan, and India

Spotted horses spread from China to Korea and Japan with no fanfare. They may have gone with ambassadors as special gifts to high officials, or they may have been taken in by some enterprising trader. So far no record of their introduction has been found. Poets and storytellers have not honored them, but artists have used them in many historic paintings. The earliest to be found so far dates from the middle of the thirteenth century, and shows the spotted horse as a trim sturdy animal. It is possible that further search will reveal more of the Japanese story. A few spotted horses have been found in Korea since 1950, but so far no mention of them has occurred in post-war Japan.

HORSES IN PASTURE. Lang Shih-ning (Giuseppe Castiglione).

One of the European missionaries active in China during the eighteenth century, the Italian Jesuit Giuseppe Castiglione (1688–1768 A.D.) occupies a unique position in the history of Chinese painting. His use of Occidental techniques of chiaroscuro, as well as his ability to use perspective to create an illusion of spatial depth in a painting, were novelties in Chinese art and greatly pleased the Chinese emperors. Both the K'ang-hsi (1662–1722 A.D.) and the Ch'ien-lung (1735–1795 A.D.) emperors employed Castiglione as a court painter. Many of his paintings portraying the horses from the Chinese imperial stables are included in the collection of Chinese art treasures now on the island of Taiwan.

Nomadic horsemen have invaded India through Afghanistan and the Kyber Pass since prehistoric times. Historic invasions include those by Darius I of Persia, Alexander of Macedon, and others, such as the Moguls in the thirteenth century A.D. Spotted horses may have come with any of these armies, but no sure record of their presence exists before the period of the Mogul painters in the late sixteenth century, when they appear in paintings, illuminated manuscripts, and tapestries.

Several photographs of Indian state processions in the nineteenth century show rajahs mounted on white horses with black spots. When Prime Minister Nehru visited in the northern hill country in 1949 he was given, on at least one occasion, a spotted horse to ride. Since only the best would do for such an important visitor, this indicates that the spotted horse still rates as a special mount in northern India.

Spotted Horses in Persia

In Persia evidence indicating the presence of spotted horses is both earlier and more abundant. The Persian plateau passed from one conqueror to another until the Moslems came in from the south in 640 A.D. In a few years Persia was entirely under the control of the invaders, whose capital was far away at Baghdad. Persian culture underwent a drastic change. All Persian scholars were forced to use the Arabic script and to study the sacred writings of Mohammed in the Arabic tongue. Under this oppressive foreign domination the Persians clung stubbornly to their own literature, legends, and art forms. In spite of Mohammed's specific teachings, they continued to show both men and animals in their art work. Of course, there are gaps in the record of Persian art, but extant art objects produced from the sixth

MINIATURE, BATTLE BETWEEN GAV AND TALHAND. MS. 239, Folio 430, *Shah Namah* of Muhammad Juki, *ca.* 1440. Courtesy of the Royal Asiatic Society, London. Photograph Courtesy of the Trustees of the British Museum, London.

The end of the fourteenth century and the beginning of the fifteenth saw the conquest of Persia by the Mongol hordes from the east under Timur the Lame, or Tamerlane. These Timurid rulers of Persia, for all their thirst for blood in wartime, were great patrons of the arts, and a flourishing school of miniature painters grew up under their patronage. A new style of the art of the miniature was developed, distinguished from earlier paintings by a greater naturalism, a greater emphasis on elements of landscape, the use of much brilliant color, and greater action in the composition of the picture, as in this battle scene, where two armies clash in a great melee. This copy of the *Shah Namah* of Firdausi was made about 1440 for the son of a Timurid shah by an artist from the school of Herat. The horses in this painting exhibit a variety of markings, including several of the "blanket" type characteristic of the present-day Appaloosa. They also recall the markings on the tomb figurines from Sinkiang, several centuries earlier.

HEIJI MONOGATARI ("The Burning of the Sanjo Palace"). Detail of Scroll. Courtesy of the Museum of Fine Arts, Boston.

One of the great achievements in Japanese art was the development of the narrative scroll. This specialized format, which enabled the artist to present a kaleidoscopic sequence of events separated both in time and space in a single work, reached the climax of its development in the twelfth and thirteenth centuries. This scroll depicts the burning of the Sanjo Palace and the capture of the ex-Emperor Shirakawa, an incident in the Heiji war of 1159 which began the struggle between the Taira and Minamota families for political control of Japan. The rearing horse in this detail provides an excellent example of the Japanese artists' ability to depict the clamor and confusion of battle. In the three scrolls of the Heiji Monogatari extant, horses with spotted coats appear frequently.

SYRIAN MAMLUK VASE. Courtesy of the Metropolitan Museum of Art, New York City, Rogers Fund, 1941.

Glass making belongs properly within the realm of the "minor arts," but during the Mamluk Period of Islamic art in the fourteenth and fifteenth centuries A.D., the technique and practice of glass blowing and the decoration of glass objects were brought to a perfection achievable by only those who are major artists in their field. This bottle of greenish glass was made around 1320. After the bottle was blown, the polychrome decoration of warriors on spotted mounts was applied in a paste of powdered glass and then gilded. The vase was then fired to fix the enamel. A fourteenth-century traveler reported that when he visited the glass market at Aleppo he could not make up his mind to leave.

century A.D. to the present show spotted horses. Here again is an indication that such horses were common in Persia long before this time.

The spotted horse also plays an important part in Persian legend, which tells of the exploits of Rustam, the great hero of the country, who presumably lived about 400 B.C. The stories of Rustam were told throughout the land for centuries by the traveling storytellers, and sometimes they were recorded in the old manuscripts. Finally they attracted the attention of Persia's greatest poet, who embodied them in one of the great epics of all time. This poet was Firdausi, and his epic poem, the *Shah Namah*, was finished about 998 A.D. The following story is taken from an English translation of the *Shah Namah* of Firdausi.[29]

Rustam, at fifteen, had reached his full stature. He was a strong, active youth, much larger and heavier than any of the other Persians. On account of his illustrious father, and a few feats of strength, the young man was chosen to lead the Persian armies against an invading Tartar host. He readily accepted the task, asking only that he be given weapons suitable to his strength, and a horse that could carry his bulk.

His father, Zal, commander in chief of the Persian armies, sent out a call for the best horses in the country. He promised a large sum of gold to the man whose horse

[29] Firdausi, *Shah Namah*, translated by A. G. and E. Warner, I, 378–381.

was chosen by the young warrior, and set the first day of the Festival of Roses for the great horse show. Many of the horse breeders regarded the honor of supplying Rustam with a horse as important as the monetary reward. Some of them had been grooming choice colts for two or three years in anticipation of this event. They swarmed in with their best to await Rustam's choice.

News of the great show, with its golden prize, spread far beyond the borders of Persia and brought choice horses from all the nearby countries, including Arabia. Such a gathering of notable steeds surpassed any in past history. The great plain before the city was covered with thousands of choice animals, waiting for the decision of the young prince.

Early on the morning of the appointed day Rustam stationed himself by the western gate with his father. A troop of cavalry formed an avenue along which the horses were led, one by one. Each horse that caught Rustam's eye was halted briefly. The young man placed his hand on the animal's back and pressed down with all his might. Each horse in turn collapsed under the pressure, "until its belly touched the ground." The strongest and best of Persia, Arabia, Afghanistan, and the steppes toward the Caspian Sea failed the test and quailed beneath Rustam's iron hand.

> At length a herd of spotted steeds sped by,
> Among them a grey mare, short-legged and fleet
> With a lion's chest and ears like two steel daggers,

NEHRU. Courtesy of European Pictures, New York City.

Prime Minister Nehru of India is shown riding a spotted horse to attend the opening of the Indian legislature in 1949.

Her breast and shoulders full, and barrel fine.
Behind her came a colt as tall as she,
His buttocks and his breast as broad as hers,
Dark eyed and tapering—a spotted bay
With belly hard, and jet black hoofs of steel,
His whole form beautiful, and his spots
Like roses spread upon a ground of saffron.

He could discern the tiny emmet's foot
Upon black cloth at night two leagues away;
Had elephantine strength with camel's stature,
And pluck of lions bred on Mount Bitsun.
Now Rustem gazing on the mare observed the elephan-
    tine colt
And coiled his lasso to catch it, but the ancient herdsman
    cried
"O chief, forbear to take another's charger."
"Whose?" Rustem asked. "The thighs have not been
    branded."
The herdsman answered, "Never mind his brand.
There are all kinds of rumors as to him.
We call him Rakush. He is a spotted bay,
As good as water and as bright as fire.
We call him Rustem's Rakush, but know of none
To master him. He has been fit to saddle
These three years. All the nobles have observed him
But at the sight of noose and cavalier,
The dam is like a lion. We cannot tell,
O chief of paladins, the reason why,
But, as a prudent man forbears to fight a dragon,
We avoid this mare when in fighting humor,
For she will rend the hearts of lions and the hides of pards."

The old man's sayings opened Rustem's eyes.
He cast his royal lasso and entangled the colt's head.
Then, like a furious elephant, the dam advanced
As she would tear off Rustem's who roared
As savage lions roar, and scared her. Then with one buffet
On the withers sent her all trembling to the ground.
She arose, sprang back, then turned and joined the herd,
While mighty Rustem stood firm, and drew the lasso
Tighter still, and laid his hand upon the colt's back,
Which gave not. Thou hast said, "It is not felt."

The hero thought, "This is the mount for me.
Now I can act." He mounted. Swift as the wind
The ruddy steed sped with him. He inquired,
"What is this Dragon's price, or who can tell it?"
"If thou art Rustem," said the herd, "redress Iran
Upon his back. Its broad champaign shall be his price;
Then thou will right the world."

Rustem saddled Rakush, and giving him rein
Observed his courage, strength, and blood,
And that he could bear rider, arms, and mail.
The spotted horse grew so precious that at night
They burned wild rue to right and left of him
For fear of harm. "They practice sorcery," thou woudst
    have said.
In flight no deer was swifter.
He was soft-mouthed, foam scattering, light in hand,
With rounded buttocks, clever and well paced.
The gallant rider and his new-found steed
Made Zal's heart joyful as the jocund spring.
He opened his treasury door, gave out dinars,
Nor recked of day or morrow.

RUSTAM CAPTURES THE KHAGAN OF CHINA.
Miniature from a shah-namah of Firdausi. Courtesy of the Metropolitan Museum, New York, Manuscript 5, gift of Alexander Smith Cochran, 1913.

The exploits of Rustam, principal hero of the great Persian epic poem the *Shah Namah* or Book of Kings, were of special importance to the people of Persia. Beginning with the conquest of the empire of Darius by Alexander the Great, Persia knew many conquerors—Greek, Islamic, Mongol, and Mughal. In the adventures in the *Shah Namah*, however, Rustam easily conquered all foreign warriors and rulers who opposed him, and even overcame supernatural foes. In this miniature, Rustam, mounted on his spotted horse Rakush, drags the khagan of China from his elephant with a lasso, greatly impairing the Chinese ruler's dignity.

The adventures of Rustam and Rakush, as recounted in the *Shah Namah* of Firdausi, fill hundreds of pages. The pair fought demons, witches, and wild beasts, as well as the human foes of Persia. Rakush was reputed to be the best war horse in the world, and responsible, to a large extent, for his master's success. With the passing years his bay coat faded to white. Then his rose spots faded too, until he looked like a white horse, but his skin was still spotted where the roses had been. He kept his strength and spirit until that dreadful day when he died with his master in a pitfall dug by Rustam's treacherous half brother.

To explain the greatness of Rakush, some of the Persians claimed he had been sired by a dwi, or demon, and the poet has Rustam call him a "dragon."[30]

In addition to his renown in war, Rakush was famous as the sire of beautiful spotted colts. When Rustam's son, Sohrab, rode forth to war, his steed was described thus:

> I have a colt, one of the breed of Rakush,
> In strength a lion, and fleet as the wind.
> He is, as 'twere, a valley-treading mountain,
> And skimmeth like a bird along the waste.
> In strength and swiftness he is like the sun.
> None ever saw so fleet a roan. Beneath
> The stamping of his feet, the bull fish quaketh.
> His leap is like the lightning. On the mountains

---

[30] *Persian Literature*, translated by James Atkinson, *World's Greatest Literature*, I, 80.

RUG. Detail. Courtesy of Dr. Francis Haines, Monmouth, Oregon.

This rug from the author's collection is dated 1912 and is a modern continuation of traditional patterns of Turkish weaving art. One element in the design of this rug is foreign to the Islamic tradition of strictly geometric nonrepresentational art—the horse. The complete pattern has four horses, all spotted, and represent Rustam's horse Rakush and Rakush's offspring who was ridden by Sohrab, Rustam's son, at their fatal encounter.

He goeth like a raven. On the water like a fish and
    water fowl.
Upon the desert like a shaft from a bow,
Pursuing and overtaking the enemy.[31]

When Sohrab fought Rustam, neither knew they were father and son. Although Sohrab and his horse held their own against the redoubtable Rustam and Rakush for one long, terrible day, Fate had willed the death of Sohrab by his father's spear.

Many ancient copies of the *Shah Namah* were illustrated by Persian painters. They usually show Rakush with spots over his whole body, but occasionally he is shown as the blanket-type spotted horse. Later artists sometimes neglected the detailed description of Firdausi and gave Rakush a pastel pink or blue color with round white spots—strictly a product of the artist's imagination.

A few Turkish artists followed the Persian practice of using men and animals in their compositions. A good example of this is a modern Turkish rug (1912) which uses the Sohrab and Rustam story, representing Rakush as a white horse with black spots, and Sohrab's mount as a red roan.

[31] Firdausi, *op. cit.*, II, 128.

Que france si   milles de londres et par belles

MINIATURE from late fifteenth-century manuscript of the *Chronicles* of Sir John Froissart. Ms. Harl. 4380, Folio 134, "The Duke of Gloucester Arrested by the Marshal and Sent to Calais." Courtesy of the Trustees of the British Museum, London.

Belgian-born Jean Froissart was in turn soldier, clerk, poet, and finally courtier to Queen Philippa, wife of England's Edward III. Froissart's *Chronicles* of England and France in the fourteenth century occupy a distinctive place in the art of historiography, for Froissart seems to have had an uncanny ability to make people talk about what they had seen and done. Commoner, statesman, soldier, and prince poured their stories into Froissart's receptive and not always critical ear. The *Chronicles* were immensely popular in manuscript editions in the fifteenth century and were one of the first works to be printed in England. This miniature, from an elaborately illuminated manuscript of the fifteenth century depicts an event that took place in 1397. Richard II rides away, supremely unconcerned, from the scene of the arrest of his uncle, the Duke of Gloucester, who is being banished to Calais for suspected treason to his nephew. One of the King's party is depicted on a spotted charger.

SPOTTED HORSES IN EUROPE

ABOUT 3,500 YEARS AGO spotted horses were domesticated somewhere on the steppes of Asia. In the intervening centuries they have spread to the far corners of the world, usually without leaving any written record of their movements. Fortunately, because these horses appeal to local artists, they were frequently used as models for sculpture, ceramics, tapestries, engravings, and paintings. A few of these art products have endured to the present time, and through them the broad outlines of the spread of the spotted horse can be traced. Year by year archeologists add to the story, but the gaps are large and numerous.

An added handicap in such a search is the failure of most writers or storytellers to mention the breed of their subject horse, and even more rarely do they give a detailed description such as that Firdausi gave for Rakush. And if the horse should be mentioned by a term common to the storyteller's audience, the details are inadequate for an understanding of just what kind of horse is meant; hence the great importance of the work of artists who presumably drew horses like those they had seen. Here then is the story of the spotted horse in early Europe as pieced out by the few pictures which have been preserved.

About 1000 B.C. a nomadic tribe from the steppes moved west along the Danube River.[1] One of their few settlements was near a large salt deposit in Austria. All traces of their buildings have vanished long ago, and the Austrian village of Hallstatt now occupies the site, but the ancient cemetery of the nomadic people was found intact, with a wealth of objects in the graves of the more important people. From these objects the archeologists have recognized that the nomads possessed a distinctive

[1] A. L. Kroeber, *Anthropology* (rev. ed.), pp. 730–731.

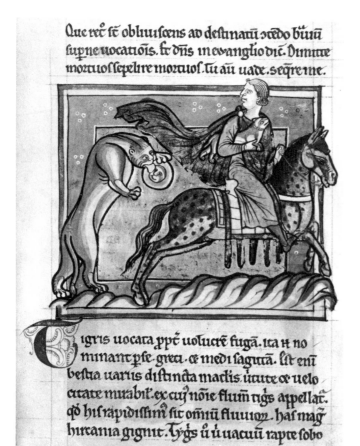

TIGER. From the Worksop Bestiary, Ms. 81, Folio 35. Courtesy of the Pierpont Morgan Library, New York City.

Bestiaries, collections of fables and bits of popular animal lore, were a very popular class of illuminated manuscripts in England in the twelfth and thirteenth centuries. Usually associated with herbals, similar collections of information about plants, they

culture. It is characterized by swords, daggers, and wagons of distinctive design, whose presence in other areas enables the archeologist to identify the influence of the nomads of Hallstatt. So far, traces of this culture have been found from Denmark to northern Italy.

A choice find in the graveyard at Hallstatt was a sword dated about 800 B.C. It was encased in a well-made scabbard of iron. The flat side of the scabbard was decorated with a line of four horsemen in single file, each one mounted on a horse with a spotted rump.

In Italy the earliest picture of a spotted horse is in an Etruscan tomb, dated about 800 B.C.[2] Since the Etruscans had come from Asia Minor about a century and a half earlier by ship, it is possible either that they found the spotted horse in Italy upon their arrival or that they imported it with them from Asia Minor.

[2] Mary Hamilton Swindler, *Ancient Painting*, Plate 387.

were among the few types of secular books produced by scribes in the Middle Ages. The information in these books was partly derived from the *Etymologiae* of Saint Isidore of Seville, a medieval "encyclopedia," and from the *Physiologiae*, an earlier medieval collection of pieces of natural history taken from classical sources written at Alexandria, and partly from Pliny. In this miniature the wily rider of the spotted horse has stolen a tiger cub, leaving a mirror to delude the mother into believing that her own image is her cub, while the thief escapes unpursued.

This bestiary was given to Worksop Priory by a canon of the Cathedral of Lincoln in 1187.

THE HALLSTATT SCABBARD. Photograph by H. Meroth, Vienna. Courtesy of the Prehistorisches Sammlung des Naturhistorisches Museum, Vienna, Austria.

After nineteenth-century excavations in the prehistoric cemetery near Hallstatt, Austria, revealed to archeologists the beginnings of Iron Age technology in northern Europe the site became the namesake for the culture of Europe north of the Alps in this period. At Hallstatt the amber trade from the north met the metal trade from the south, while extensive salt mines in the area brought in additional wealth, as shown by the elaborate grave goods of the Hallstatt burials. One grave yielded this iron scabbard, dated *ca.* 800 B.C., a product of the new metallurgical knowledge brought into Europe from Anatolia. The people of Hallstatt were members of the groups of nomadic horsemen from the Asian steppes who had invaded Europe in the second millennium B.C. The more civilized peoples of the Mediterranean called these people "barbarians" indiscriminately, but in western Asia and Russia these nomads are usually called "Scythians" and the people of Western Europe "Celts." Traces of both Scythian animal art and the intricately interlaced designs of later Celtic are evident in the decoration of this scabbard, as well as a representation of two "barbarian" customs introduced by these people—riding horseback and wearing long trousers.

MINIATURE FROM VELISLAVOVA BIBLE. Courtesy of the University Library, Prague, Czechoslovakia. MS. XXIII C 124. Folio 77 a.

Another evidence of the spread of spotted horses to eastern Europe is found in this miniature from the Velislavova Bible, dating from around 1340. Sixteen miniatures, lightly colored, in this one book contain representations of spotted horses. Several centuries later spotted horses appear in Bohemian and Moravian folk art. In particular they are associated with some of the saints most popular with folk painters—St. Isidore and St. Wencelas, the patron saint of Bohemia.

So far the art and literature of the Roman Empire have produced only one definite reference to a spotted-horse type. In the third century A.D. the poet Oppian lists a spotted breed which he calls the "Orynx," and says that the spots are produced by branding the foals with hot irons.[3] It is evident from his text that he has not seen these horses, but has heard of them.

After the collapse of the Roman Empire Europe passed through a troubled period lasting for centuries. The monasteries were the chief centers of learning. Here tapestries and illuminated manuscripts were produced and preserved. In addition, the walls of some of the chapels and churches were decorated with frescoes. All of these are art forms which can be preserved even during times of strife. The tapestries and manuscripts can be stored in chests or vaults, and the frescoes will endure as long as the building is intact.

From the eighth century spotted horses appear on many of these art forms produced from Constantinople on the east to Spain on the west. They appear as far north as England, Denmark, and Scandinavia, and were used in most of these areas through the nineteenth century. Usually the spotted horse is shown as the mount for a distinguished person, indicating that this type of horse was much used by people of rank and wealth. In following pages more detail will be given on spotted horses in Austria, Germany, Scandinavia, France, England, and Spain.

[3] Anderson, *op. cit.*, p. 21.

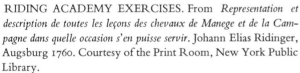

RIDING ACADEMY EXERCISES. From *Representation et description de toutes les leçons des chevaux de Manege et de la Campagne dans quelle occasion s'en puisse servir.* Johann Elias Ridinger, Augsburg 1760. Courtesy of the Print Room, New York Public Library.

The seeds of *haute ecole*, the ultimate in the art of riding, are found in Xenophon's famous treatise on horsemanship of the fourth century B.C., in which the various military exercises taught to war horses are considered as spectacles as well as military tactics. In the Middle Ages equestrianism was an important subject in the education of a knight, and the various leaps and maneuvers taught cavalry horses were devastating when used upon dis-

mounted troops. When gunpowder and modern weapons put an end to the practical value of these exercises, equitation remained a highly valued art, largely because of its snob appeal. During the sixteenth and seventeenth centuries a large number of manuals of equitation were written and schools were founded, often under the patronage of a ruler or nobleman, to teach the ancient skills of riding and training horses to the sons of the aristocracy. The basic exercises and their variations which were developed then have remained the basis of "high school" riding to this day. The exercises performed by the spotted horses in these eighteenth-century engravings are still in the repertory of the Spanish Riding School in Vienna.

This young tiger-horse, at Oranien-Polder, not far from the town of Delft, Holland, was marked with this sheaf bouquet in black, like the other spots. High nobles of Schlesien, Germany, purchased this extreme rarity on their trip to Holland, in 1743, at an enormous price.

ENGRAVINGS OF TWO HORSES by Johann Elias Ridinger. (*Above, and opposite page.*) Courtesy of the Print Room, The New York Public Library, New York City.

Johann Elias Ridinger was born in Ulm, Germany in 1698, the son of a writer who was also a dilletante painter. Ridinger was trained from an early age to become a professional artist. In his teens he studied with a famous animal painter of Augsburg, Johann Falch; and it is possible that he also studied under J. G. Hamilton, the famous animal painter of the Viennese court. Although he was himself a painter, Ridinger is best known for the engravings, either his original work or after earlier paintings, which illustrate many volumes on hunting, riding, and the schooling of horses. He died in 1760.

An oil painting in the Spanische Reitschule in Vienna depicts a horse remarkably similar to the Ridinger subject.

CHIEF HANDPRINT. Courtesy of Burmeister's Handprint Farms, Pontiac, Michigan.

Anno 1740.

Ist dyses noble Pferd so ein Schimel mit liecht und dunckel braunen
auch grauen Flecken gesprengt, mit Schwarzen extremiteten an Ohren
Maul und Schencklen gezeichnet in dem Kaÿserl. Reitstall zu Wien
nach dem Leben gemahlt worden.

Aug: Querfurth. pinx.   I. El. Ridinger Sc: et excud.

[This beautiful animal, a white horse sprinkled with light and dark brown, and even grey, spots,
with black ears, mouth, and shanks, is represented in the Emperor's stable at Vienna and painted
according to life.]

Spotted Horses in Austria, Germany, and Scandinavia

Since the discovery of the Hallstatt scabbard with its spotted horses no other representations earlier than the twelfth century A.D. have been found in Central Europe.[4] During this period of about two thousand years there is no evidence either for or against the presence of spotted horses in this area, although one item indicates the probability of such horses. The nomads from the steppes made attacks from time to time. Presumably they would bring in some spotted stock, and might leave a few behind. There is no indication that the horses shown on the early tapestries are recent arrivals, and from the twelfth century on these spotted horses appear rather regularly.

About the middle of the sixteenth century spotted horses became more important in Austria, as a result of the growth of the House of Habsburg. The empire of Charles V included both Spain and Austria, as well as many other areas. When he abdicated in 1555 he gave Spain to his son, Philip II, and Austria to his younger brother, Ferdinand. Thus the sovereigns of these two powerful countries were close relatives, as well as being allies in various wars. They exchanged rich gifts of various kinds from time to time.

Possibly such a gift was the group of Andalusian stallions and mares which Ferdinand secured about 1560.[5]

These animals were placed on a breeding farm at Kladrub, Bohemia, for a few years. Then the bulk of them were moved to Equile Lipizzano,[6] at the head of the Adriatic Sea on the limestone hill pastures east of Trieste. Soon the horses from this stud became known as Lipizzans, and for many years were raised chiefly to furnish mounts for the Austrian royal family. A contemporary painting of the mares at this stud shows that many of them were spotted.

At Vienna special training was given to horses which showed unusual intelligence and tractability. Soon this school was taking only Lipizzan horses, and, since these were of Spanish stock, it became known as the Spanish Riding School.[7] Many pictures of horses in this school about the middle of the eighteenth century show all of them spotted.

While Maria Theresa was ruler of Austria, 1740–1780, the stud at Lipizzano reached its greatest size, with about 350 horses.[8] About 200 of these were brood mares. All the stallions showing special aptitude for the Spanish School training were sent to Vienna. The rest, except for the breeding stock, were distributed to nobles serving with the armies. This accounts for the many battle pictures in which one or two of the officers are mounted on spotted horses.

---

[4] Betty Kurth, *Die Deutschen Bilderpiche des Mittelalters*, Band I, abb. 14, p. 4.

[5] Mathilde Windisch-Graetz, *The Spanish Riding School*, p. 7.

[6] Beverley M. Bowie, "The White Horses of Vienna," *National Geographic*, CXIV, No. 3 (September, 1958), 401–419.

[7] *Ibid.*

[8] Windisch-Graetz, *op. cit.*, p. 8.

THE STUD AT LIPIZZANO. By Johann Georg Hamilton. Detail. Photography by Walt Disney Productions, Ltd., Vienna. Courtesy of Colonel Alois Podhajsky, Commandant, Spanische Reitschule, Vienna.

Johann Georg Hamilton, the most famous horse and animal painter of the Habsburg court in the eighteenth century, was born of Scottish parentage in Brussels in 1672. Around the opening of the eighteenth century he came to Vienna, where his paintings of hunting scenes, horses, and hounds were extremely popular with the numerous princes of the Empire. His work was in great demand for the decorating of hunting lodges such as the Jagdschloss Ohrad and the Summer Palace at Rennwege near Vienna. When Prince Adam Franz von Schwarzenberg became emperor, he made Hamilton court painter. Hamilton's reputation as an unsurpassed painter of horses made him the natural choice to paint the stud of the famous Spanish Riding School of Vienna at Lippizano, a small village near Trieste. This school, founded by Duke Charles of Styria in 1580, was beyond question the most famous of continental schools of equitation. Through the years continual imports of stock from Spain preserved the quality of the original Andalusian breed of the original stud. This group of brood mares, painted in 1727, shows the great number of coat colors prevalent among the original Lippizaner stock—palomino, tobiano, and well-marked blanketed Appaloosa.

These horses are dark when foaled. Many of them are dappled grey at the age of three, fading to white in three or four more years. The managers of the breeding farm at Lipizzano have developed a strain of white horses.

Of the spotted horses left at Kladrub, some were crossed with stockier animals to provide carriage horses.[9] About this time the Archbishop of Salzburg, not far to the west, acquired some spotted horses,[10] probably from Kladrub. He crossed these with heavier stock and produced a spotted work horse described as built like a good little Belgian. These horses were popular in the mountain valleys south of Salzburg, especially in Pinzgau Valley. In time the spotted carriage horses of Austria became known as the Pinzgau horses, although many of them must have come from Kladrub.

During the seventeenth century the Austrian court set the style for much of the court life of Europe until it was finally overshadowed by the Grand Monarch, Louis XIV of France. It is probable that the use of spotted horses by the Austrian royal family was the chief reason for the increased importance of the spotted stock in the royal stables of Denmark. In 1671 the royal riding school received a spotted horse from the breeding farm, and in 1680 Christian V presented a team of six spotted horses to his sister Ulrikke Eleanora.[11]

At Fredrikborg, King Christian VI set aside a special section in 1745 for the spotted horses. Some outstanding horses were produced here in the next years. Then for some unexplained reason the Danes had difficulty in finding mares of the right color and conformation, and the number of spotted horses declined rapidly.

Then in the Napoleonic wars a battalion of Spanish troops served in Denmark. In 1808 a Danish butcher bought a spotted mare from them. This was the famous Flaebe mare, and her offspring started the excellent Knabstrupper line, which was the principal strain of spotted horses in Denmark during the nineteenth century.[12] Several of these horses, famous for their speed, were ridden by Danish officers in the Schleswig War of 1848–1850. The Knabstruppers have diminished in numbers and importance during the twentieth century, being replaced by machines.

As early as the eighth century Vikings in Norway carved the heads of two spotted horses in whalebone (British Museum Collections), and in the twelfth century Norwegians produced a tapestry with a rider on a spotted horse. A few more art objects with such horses are found in Scandinavia during the next six centuries; then the folk artists take over. During the late eighteenth and the early nineteenth century a large number of paintings are to be seen in Sweden, usually on Biblical motifs, with spotted horses in abundance. Here, among

[9] Ibid.
[10] Pedersen, op. cit., p. 1.   [11] Ibid., p. 2.
[12] Ibid., p. 2.

WALL PAINTING from Skibby Church, Sealand, Denmark. Courtesy of the Nationalmuseet, Copenhagen, Denmark.

The tradition of decorating the walls and ceilings of churches with frescoes was as strong in Scandinavia as it was in Italy. Many of the same themes were equally popular in both north and south, and this fifteenth-century scene of the Triumph of Death from the Chancel of Skibby Church, Sealand, Denmark, has its counterpart in many Italian churches. The three kings, each on a spotted mount, ride forth with their falcons for a day's sport. They symbolize the vanities of life. To the right, the same three kings reappear as skeletons consumed by gigantic worms. Spotted horses are found in numerous other wall paintings from Danish churches of this period. In the same fresco in which the three kings appear, St. Martin, riding a spotted horse, divides his cloak with a beggar.

the mounts of Joseph's eleven brothers are five spotted ones. Sometimes one of the Three Wise Men rides a spotted horse; sometimes all three of them are so mounted. Several other Biblical and religious personalities ride or drive spotted horses.

Although spotted horses are prominent in Swedish art, there is no evidence for Swedish breeding such as was established in Austria and in Denmark. Diana Von Shinkel,[13] of Hallansberg, Sweden, reports that there is a spotted strain in the Gothland pony and that her grandmother raised some spotted horses in the Moholm district of Sweden. Of course many of the soldiers in the armies of Gustavus Adolphus and Charles XII could have seen spotted horses as they campaigned in Central Europe.

Spotted Horses in France and England

Spotted horses appear in French art by the middle of the eleventh century, and are fairly common thereafter. Usually such a horse is shown carrying a king, noble, or saint. Hence it is obvious that such horses, although possibly scarce and reserved for the upper classes, were known to the painters. A thirteenth-century French artisan depicted a highly stylized spotted horse in the bronze aquamanile illustrated here.

So far there has been no record found of a French es-

[13] Diana Von Shinkel, letter to the author, Hallansberg, Moholen, Sweden, August 5, 1958.

AQUAMANILE. French bronze. Courtesy of the Metropolitan Museum of Art, New York, Rogers Fund, 1910.

Perhaps because the spotted horse is a somewhat exotic animal, the French Gothic artisan who made this aquamanile in the shape of a centaur chose to give the equine half a spotted hide. The human half represents a crowned figure who holds with one hand the head of a grotesque feathered creature with a long snakelike neck which serves as a spout. This thirteenth-century bronze is an example of ecclesiastical art and was used to hold water for services of the church. Medieval aquamaniles were frequently made in the form of animals, to combine function and decoration, as the four feet served as a base and the head as a spout.

Czarniecki crossing the Vistula River at Płock.

Czarniecki crossing a sea inlet.

WATERCOLORS by Juliusz Kossak. Courtesy of the National Museum, Warsaw, Poland.

Whatever may have been the principal source for the breeding of spotted horses in Europe, there is no doubt that they spread throughout the continent, from Spain north to Scandinavia and east to Poland. Poland's prolific nineteenth-century painter of horses, Juliusz Kossak, portrayed the leopard-spotted variety often in his water colors of genre scenes or subjects from Polish history. Kossak was an art student in Paris in the 1850's, when the Impressionist school was at its beginning, but he chose to return to Poland and to develop an individual art combining the water-color technique he had perfected in Paris with a patriotic desire to keep the great moments of Polish history alive for his countrymen. There is a definite Polish character to the numerous water colors with luminous coloring in which Kossak depicts the glittering, knightly life of the castles and cities of the Poland of an earlier age.

tablishment for breeding spotted horses such as were found in both Austria and Denmark. It is possible that the French imported their horses from the Netherlands or from southern Germany. Dutch and Flemish artists used such horses in paintings from the fifteenth century on.

In the second half of the seventeenth century, when spotted horses were fashionable at the courts of Austria and Denmark, Louis XIV ordered both paintings and tapestries showing him on spotted mounts. His successor, Louis XV, was similarly portrayed.

Louis XVI used a matched pair of spotted horses as a driving team. These may have been a present from his mother-in-law, Maria Theresa of Austria, who had a large herd of Lipizzans at this time. This team was used to take the king to hunting meets, as this account demonstrates: "5 August 1777, the King [Louis XVI] hunted the wild boar with the hounds of M. le Duc [Prince de Conde]. He drove to the meet 'avec un attelage de chevaux tigres, dont la robe est fort belle'."[14] It is curious that both the French and the Danes call these animals "tiger" horses, rather than "leopard."

Since the Napoleonic Wars spotted horses have not been common in France. Most of them are found in circuses, and are imported from Central Europe.

In England the pattern is much like that in France. Spotted horses are found in illuminated manuscripts as

[14] Sacheverell Sitwell, *The Hunters and the Hunted*, p. 61 n.

BALDISHOL TAPESTRY. Courtesy of the Kunstindustri-museet, Oslo, Norway.

This tapestry of Norwegian make was found between the floors of the Church of Baldishol in Norway. Woven of linen and wool, it dates from the late twelfth or early thirteenth century, and is considered the most important example of early Norwegian weaving extant. Authorities believe that this tapestry shows traces of Eastern influence which may have come into the West with the returning Crusaders. Norway, like other countries of Viking origin, has long had constant trade connections with the East and Near East via the Varangian Empire in Russia and Constantinople.

DOESBURG
Ville au Comté de Zutphen, sur le quel de Drusus a rendroit où ce
canal entre dans l'Issel Le Roy l'assiegea luy même en personne Cest a ce siege qu'il
prit soin de la reduction de vingt places fameuses des Hollandois &c. pour celle cy en
deux jours de tranchées & la garnison qui estoit de quatre mille hommes se rendit a discretion
Le 21 Juin 1672

CROSSING THE RHINE. Adam Frans van der Meulen. Courtesy of the Musée National du Louvre, Paris.

Adam Frans van der Meulen was born in Flanders in 1632 and studied under Pieter Snayers, a celebrated painter of martial scenes. Van der Meulen was brought to Paris in 1667 by Colbert, the Minister of Finance to Louis XIV, as part of the government-directed program to stimulate the arts in France. Louis was so pleased by the Flemish painter's battle scenes that he ordered Van der Meulen to accompany the French armies on their campaigns as a sort of war correspondent. Although such details as topography and military equipment are extremely accurate in Van der Meulen's work, he showed only the color and pageantry of warfare, not the brutal realities of battle and death. This painting records an incident in the early course of the war against the Dutch that France waged from 1672 to 1678. Van der Meulen is best represented by the series of twenty canvases in the Louvre, enormous in size and heroic in scope, which he executed to perpetuate the military glories of the Sun King. The monarch is seen on a spotted charger, receiving reports and grandly gesturing with his baton.

LOUIS XIV AT THE SIEGE OF DOESBURG. Courtesy of the J. B. Speed Museum, Louisville, Kentucky.

The establishment of large government-sponsored factories for the production of tapestries was an important factor in the program, initiated by Colbert, Minister of Finance to Louis XIV, to develop the economy of France. While the Gobelin factory was established to make tapestries for the royal palaces and residences, the Beauvais factory established in 1664 was a commercial enterprise. Known principally for floral and decorative work on a small scale, the Beauvais weavers also produced series of pictorial tapestries such as this portrait of Louis XIV at the siege of Doesburg. This commemorates another incident in the war with the Dutch, one that took place about one week after the crossing of the Rhine by the armies of France shown in the painting by Adam Frans van der Meulen. As the inscription on the tapestry recounts, Louis personally conducted the siege which captured the fortress of Doesburg with its garrison of four thousand men. As in the Van der Meulen work, Louis is shown mounted on a spotted horse, evidently his favorite breed of war horse.

early as the twelfth century, usually carrying saints or nobles. The first record of a specific spotted horse dates from the reign of Charles II. About 1685 a grey horse with red on his rump was brought in from abroad, and was named, tersely and descriptively, "Bloody Buttocks"!

Forty-eight years later the English Stud Book lists another Bloody Buttocks, possibly a descendant of the first one. This horse produced a son, Bay Bloody Buttocks. It is possible that Oxford's Bloody-Shouldered Arabian, listed in 1710, belongs to this line.[15]

A few spotted horses show up in English paintings in the eighteenth and nineteenth centuries, for instance a painting of a British spotted stallion by John Wootton, (1677–1765), from a collection of the late Earl of Coventry. Also a few breeders were raising such horses, which were sometimes known as "Chubarry," a name borrowed from Spain, or "Blagdon," from an English breeding farm.

In recent years the publicity concerning the Appaloosa horse in America stimulated a few English horsemen to form a British Spotted Horse Society.[16] Although it has not been very active, some interest in the Appaloosa does exist in England, and a casual traveler can still find a few spotted horses in the English countryside.

[15] John Hervey, *Racing in America, 1665–1865*, Chart 2.
[16] Sir Phys Llewellyn, Bart., "The British Spotted Horse," a pamphlet prepared by the British Spotted Horse Society; reprinted from *Riding* (October, 1949).

Spotted Horses in Spain

About 875 B.C., a Phoenician colony was located on the coast of northern Africa where the land juts out toward Sicily. Blessed with a good harbor and a monopoly of the western Mediterranean trade, this colony, Carthage, grew and prospered until it dominated the whole western Mediterranean area. Carthaginian ships even sailed beyond the Pillars of Hercules to Britain and the Baltic. Gradually the growing city state encroached on the Greek colonies in Sicily until Rome drove her from that island in the First Punic War. Carthage then turned her energies to the Spanish peninsula and rapidly expanded her small coastal holdings into an empire. To protect her valuable new possessions, her general, Hamilcar, built up a highly efficient army, with special emphasis on the cavalry.

Spain had a large number of horses brought in across the Pyrenees from Gaul. The Carthaginians sent in many fine stallions from northern Africa to improve the stock, and encouraged the natives to raise a large number of horses. Thus the horses of Spain were bred from some of the best stock available in the Mediterranean world and could trace their ancestry back through many centuries and many generations to the horses of central Asia.

Finally Rome, in the long, bitter Second Punic War, defeated Carthage and took over the Spanish peninsula. For centuries after the conquest, horses from Spain were

FOUR HORSEMEN from a Beatus *Commentary*. Ms. Add. 11695, Folio 102 v. Courtesy of the Trustees of the British Museum, London.

This miniature is an illustration from a copy of the *Commentary* of Saint Beatus de Liebana written about 776 A.D. on the Apocalypse of St. John, a favorite work of Spanish scribes of the late ninth to twelfth centuries. About twenty-five Beatus manuscripts of this period survive today as treasures of the libraries which own them. In Spain of this period, Visigoth, Jewish, Arab, Berber, Byzantine, Syrian, and Persian cultures met, and each contributed something to the unique character of Spanish art and culture. Perhaps it was the influence of the Moslem love of decoration displayed in mosques and in the Alhambra which led the unknown artist of this miniature to depict spotted rather than plain horses. Or perhaps, after painting the seven-headed, hundred-eyed monsters of the *Apocalypse*, an everyday horse would not seem appropriate.

4.

prized in Rome for their speed, which popular superstition at the time ascribed to an unorthodox method of breeding. The west wind, fresh from the Atlantic, was supposed to cause pregnancy in any mares that faced to the east at certain periods. The colts born to such mares were of superior stock, fleet as their sire, the west wind.

From that day to this, Spain has had a reputation for breeding fine horses, but the invasion of the Goths greatly reduced the number of horses raised in the country. The conquering Goths reserved for themselves the exclusive right to own and use horses, partly as a mark of their superior status, and partly to reduce the danger of revolt. Shut in on all sides by the mountains and the sea, the Goths were safe from invasion for a long period. The absence of mounted enemies led them to breed horses for beauty and easy gaits rather than for speed, courage, and endurance. They neglected their cavalry drill and their arms.

In time the neglect of horse breeding and of horsemanship brought disaster to the country. The mounted hosts of Islam came out of Arabia, across Egypt, across Libya, racing on to the west, gaining thousands of fierce desert warriors with every advance. The water barrier at the Straits of Gibraltar halted them briefly. Then a daring raider, with a small force of well-trained, superbly mounted cavalry, crossed to Spain in search of plunder, planning a swift escape before the Spanish could muster their forces for effective pursuit. His daring raid paid off in a series of stunning victories so overwhelming that he gave up all thought of retreat to Africa. Instead, he settled in the country and sent to Africa for more Moslems to help him exploit the new conquest.

The Spanish, overwhelmed by the initial attacks, finally managed to organize small centers of resistance in the rugged mountain country in northwestern Spain. Of necessity they adopted the cavalry equipment and the cavalry tactics of the enemy. Thus while the rest of Europe was breeding massive horses to carry their heavily armored knights into battle, the Spanish were concentrating on horses of medium size, but of great agility, speed, and endurance.

One of the great breeds of Spain was the Andalusian horse. Some of the best of the Moorish-Arab stock were crossed with the heavier Vilanas from the Pyrenees[17] to produce animals of greater size and strength, which became known in time as the Andalusian. Some of these horses were spotted.

As early as 1109 A.D. spotted horses appear in Spanish art, and they keep recurring during the next three centuries. Possibly these are some of the Vilanas from the Pyrenees, which helped spot the Andalusians. One account states that some spotted horses were sent from Poland to Spain as a diplomatic gift,[18] in which case they could have strengthened the spotted strain in Spanish stock.

[17] Bowie, *op. cit.*, p. 409.
[18] Pedersen, *op. cit.*, p. 1.

When Philip II sent some Andalusians to his uncle, Ferdinand of Austria, about 1560, most of them must have been spotted to produce the animals shown in the old Austrian pictures, for there is no hint that any spotted horses from Austria were added to this Lipizzan herd.

After seven hundred years of conflict the combined armies of Castile and Aragon conquered the last of the Spanish Moors at Granada in 1492. Thus the Spanish soldiers, freed by the victory, and the Spanish horses, developed to a peak of perfection, were ready for the next great task, the conquest of the New World, discovered that year by Christopher Columbus.

SPOTTED HORSES IN NORTH AMERICA

Introduction of Spanish Horses

THE SPANISH CONQUISTADORS blazed a trail of blood and plunder across the West Indies, Peru, and Mexico, their victories made possible by the spirit and endurance of the Spanish horse. Along this trail streamed merchants, missionaries, miners, and stockmen eager to exploit the dazzling opportunities in this new land. Within a century after the first voyage of Columbus, Spanish rule was firmly established over all of Mexico. Fabulously rich silver mines and vast expanses of pasture lands insured the rapid settling of the plateau in northern Mexico, and led to the establishment of great haciendas around Durango and Chihuahua.

Since the spotted horses were common among the Andalusian stock of Spain in the sixteenth century, they were probably included in shipments to Mexico from the time of the conquest in 1519–1521, and so formed a part of the herds of Juan de Oñate in the settlement of New Mexico. There is a vague tale, too, that a shipload of spotted horses came directly from Trieste to Vera Cruz about 1621. This story cannot be verified, because the Trieste shipping records before 1776 have been lost, but such a shipment by a noble at that time probably would have come from the Lipizzan herd near the city. It would help account for the fine Appaloosas which appeared from time to time in various parts of the American west.

When Chihuahua had been settled the frontier kept moving onward. New countries beckoned the adventurous. Beyond the ranges each could hope to find vast treasures in gems and precious metals, broad fields for new ranchos, villages of docile Indians waiting to serve new masters. And so the restless surge of ambitious men pushed the frontier out and out, into the mountain valleys of New Mexico.

Vanguard of the northern movement was the expedition of Francisco Vasquez Coronado. Starting from Sinaloa in 1539, by 1542 he had completed a huge loop that enfolded New Mexico, Oklahoma, southern Kansas, and western Texas. During the same years Hernando de Soto was pushing across from Florida to the Mississippi River. His men reached the plains of Texas and narrowly missed a meeting with Coronado in the buffalo country.

A great deal of romantic nonsense has since been published about strays from the horse herds of De Soto and Coronado.[1] These few lost horses, according to some imaginative people, are supposed to have filled the Great Plains with their descendants in the course of a hundred years or so. The wild bands, started by these strays, are said to have supplied all the Indians of the buffalo country with horses through natural increase. In support of their story, writers cite the story of the Twelve Horses, freed near Buenos Aires at almost the same time, which multiplied so rapidly they soon stocked all the Pampas country.

Careful modern research has proved that the horse herds of the Argentine did not come from the famous Twelve Horses, but from stock ranches along the foothills of the Andes. Research has also proved that there were no horses, wild or tame, in the buffalo country of

Texas ninety years after Coronado passed that way. The first authentic account of the use of horses by western Indians is dated 1659,[2] and the first positive evidence of wild horses anywhere on the Great Plains does not come until 1705.[3]

Spanish Horses in New Mexico

Juan de Oñate, grandee of New Spain and distinguished citizen of the mining center of Zacatecas, was commissioned by Philip II of Spain to conquer and settle the upper valley of the Rio Grande del Norte for the greater glory of God—and greater profit to the Spanish crown. Early in the spring of the year of Our Lord 1598, Oñate led forth a mighty caravan of soldier settlers, their families, Franciscan missionaries, and many slaves, both Indian and Negro. North across the shifting desert sands they traveled, heading for the water gap where the great river broke through the mountain ranges.

Once through this gap, El Paso del Norte, they marched across the desert plateau east of the valley which held the river. Finally Juan de Oñate and his men reached the upper valley of the Rio Grande, where villages of Pueblo Indians farmed the rich alluvial soil. Here he founded his settlements, taking the local Indians as serfs to farm the fields they had once owned and to herd

---

[1] Francis Haines, "Where Did the Plains Indians Get Their Horses?" *American Anthropologist*, XL, No. 1 (January–March, 1938), 112–117; "The Northward Spread of Horses among the Plains Indians," *ibid.*, XL, No. 3 (July–September, 1938), 429–437.

[2] F. V. Scholes, "Troublous Times in New Mexico, 1659–1670," *New Mexico Historical Review*, XII (1937), 134–174.
[3] A. B. Thomas, "Spanish Expeditions Northeast of New Mexico," p. 27.

CINCHADA. F. Molino Campos. S. A. Fabrica Argentina de Alpargatas. Edward Larocque Tinker's Hall of the Horsemen of the Americas, University of Texas, Austin, Texas.

The gauchos of Argentina are among the most individualistic peoples in the world. They have much in common with the cowboy of the North American West, due to the similarities of their occupations, but civilization has not encroached on the gaucho's pampas to the extent it has upon the cowboy's lands, and isolation has tended to preserve the South American's distinctive dress, folklore and folkways. The language of the gaucho, developed to describe the tools and institutions peculiar to his livelihood, has been the subject of much study and a dictionary of gaucho terms has been published, the *Vocabulario* of Tito Saubidet. In everyday Spanish, *cinchada* means belt or saddle cinch, but to the gaucho it refers to the equestrian tug-of-war shown in this painting, in which one contestant attempts to pull his opponent across a line marked in the ground. This special language is particularly rich in words to describe types of horses and their coat patterns and colors. In Argentina the term for spotted horse is *tigre* or *pintado*. This illustration is one of a series of caricature portraits of gauchos and their customs done by F. Molino Campos, an Argentine artist, and made popular in South America by their use on calendars.

the seven thousand head of stock brought from old Mexico. The Indians of the pueblos were trapped. If they stayed, they were slaves, under harsh taskmasters. If they fled, they would be captured by the fierce, nomadic tribes that hemmed them in on every side. Usually life as a slave to a Spanish colonist seemed preferable to torture at the hands of their traditional enemies, Apache, Comanche, Navajo, and Piute.

In the Rio Grande Valley, where there was no adequate supply of fencing materials to enclose the fields, gardens and grain fields lay open to the depredations of any stray stock. As a result, all the stock was kept far from the crop lands during the growing season, with the herders vigilant day and night. All year long the Indian herders trudged wearily after the flocks, driving them to new pastures and to water, guarding constantly against predators. Eagles, coyotes, pumas, and wild Indians were constant threats. For much of the year the flocks had to be kept far from the villages, in constant search for fresh pasture. Most of the care of the sheep and goats was entrusted to the Indian men, under some supervision from the Spanish foremen.

The Spanish cattle, known in later times as the Texas longhorns, could not be herded by men on foot. Only an experienced horseman, well mounted, could cope with them, and with the horse herds. By Spanish law and Spanish policy Indians were not allowed to ride horses, a privilege reserved for Europeans. So the *vaque-ros* were Spanish, and the large herds required many of them.

Each *vaquero* needed a riding string of twelve to fifteen horses to carry on his work properly. In addition, each Spanish family needed several horses for personal use, since they had no carriage. Horses were needed too for the military patrols, and for the troops which occasionally pursued the Plains tribes. All of these horses had to be fed, watered, saddled, and looked after. Corrals and stables had to be cleaned. And all this menial work was done by Indian stable boys.

In spite of legal prohibitions and the opposition of the masters, it was inevitable that many of the stable boys would learn to ride.[4] When none of the Spanish were watching, boys would ride horses to and from the stables, to water or to pasture. Occasionally a rancher might ignore the law and send an Indian boy with an urgent message, or to round up the horse herd in a time of emergency. Sometimes the boys accompanied their masters on long trips to take care of the extra horses and to handle the camp chores.

Once these Indian stable boys had become experienced riders they were not so docile or so content with their servile status. If the master's temper flared too often, or the work load grew too heavy, the boys could

[4] Herbert Eugene Bolton, *Rim of Christendom: A Biography of Eusebio Francisco Kino, Pacific Coast Pioneer*, pp. 491–524.

LEWIS AND CLARK MEETING THE FLATHEADS AT ROSS' HOLE. Charles M. Russell. Photograph courtesy of the Historical Society of Montana, Helena.

In 1911 the State of Montana commissioned an historical mural for the wall behind the Speaker's desk in the Chamber of Representatives in the Capitol building in Helena. The commission went to Montana's best-known artist, Charles Russell. The subject selected was the event described in Meriwether Lewis' *Journal* in the entry for September 4, 1805, when, pursuing the course of the Bitterroot River, the explorers "discovered a large encampment of Indians: when we had reached them and alighted from our horses, we were received with great cordiality." The Indians were members of the Flathead tribe and the meeting took place in the present area of Montana, on the return from the Pacific coast of the expedition headed by Lewis and William Clark. Russell's mural is his own highly individual treatment of the scene. The two explorers are relegated to the background, and the foreground is devoted to a group of Indians circling and wheeling in their excitement at the advent of strangers. The Indians with their elaborate costumes and fine horses, an Appaloosa prominent among them, dominate the painting as they did Russell's imagination.

choose the best of the horses in their charge and be far across the desert before their flight was discovered.

Sometimes the runaways bettered their lot by such bold action, but there was always the danger of a worse fate. Always they risked death or further enslavement at the hands of Navajo or Apache. The more fortunate fugitives were adopted by one of the wild tribes, where their horses and horsemanship might give them positions of leadership. Whether slave or leader in his new group, the ex-stable boy became an instructor in the care and use of horses. Thus Spanish horses and Spanish customs regarding them spread in ever widening circles far beyond the settlements of New Mexico.

The Apache never really adopted the horse as a servant. They valued the animal chiefly for food. But in the buffalo country horses were too valuable to eat. Instead they were treasured and protected. In time of danger they were taken into the tipi, even if some of the family had to sleep outside. As the Plains Indians never became horse breeders of any importance, many new animals had to be stolen each year from the Spanish ranches.

Horses for the Plains Indians

Occasionally Indians from the Plains tried to buy horses from the Spanish settlements, but the Spanish officials strictly enforced the laws against such traffic. While dried buffalo meat and tanned robes were acceptable as payment for ordinary goods, they could not be traded for horses.

In an effort to discourage runaway slaves, the Spanish offered to buy them back from any tribe managing to capture them. At first the Indians accepted cloth and weapons for such captives, but they soon realized that Christian Indians had a special value to the missionaries, and refused to surrender them except for horses. Since the missionaries could not bear to lose their converts to the heathen, they induced the civil authorities to suspend the law in such special cases. The early records show that some Spanish settlers, captured in raids, were also ransomed for horses.[5]

Thus by barter, trade, and theft, the Plains tribes built up their horse herds, but it was a slow process. A drouth might ruin the pasture, or a blizzard wipe out a large part of the herd. Wolves and pumas took their toll. In times of famine, some of the poorer horses would be sacrificed to save the people from starvation. By 1680 only those tribes near the Spanish settlements had adapted themselves to the horse.

The Pueblo Revolt of 1680 changed the picture. For eighty years the Indians had bowed before the might of the Spanish conquerors, but resentment grew with the passing years. Harsh treatment, forced labor, and strict laws against the ancient religious ceremonies in the kivas finally brought on the explosion. Under the leadership of Popé, a deposed medicine man, the Indians of northern New Mexico arose on the same day and killed some four hundred of the Spanish. About twenty-five hundred

[5] Thomas, *loc. cit.*

COWBOY WORKING CATTLE. Edward Borein. Courtesy of Mrs. Helen de Mott, Santa Barbara, California.

To most of the artists who depicted the spotted horse, the spectacular markings of the animal were of primary importance. These were the qualities that made them favorites for parade and show horses. To the professional horseman, whether breeder or cowboy, other considerations were more important. Versatility, endurance, and temperament all came before looks in determining the esteem a mount would hold in the eyes of a cowboy, though doubtless no cowpoke objected to owning or riding a horse that caught the eye. Ed Borein was both a cowboy and an artist, a combination that enabled him to know a good cow horse when he saw it and to paint it as well.

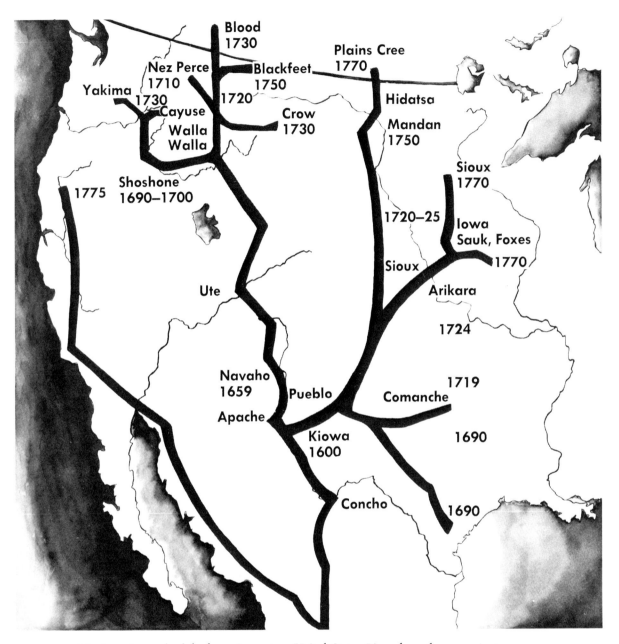

Northward spread of the horse in western United States. Lines show the approximate routes followed by the horses; dates indicate the approximate time the horse reached each area. From *The American Anthropologist*, Volume XL, Number 3 (July–September, 1938), p. 430.

more escaped to the south, and congregated at El Paso, but they had lost their homes, their farms, and their herds.

To the Pueblo Indians the captured sheep represented real wealth, since these animals fitted into the Indian economy. Sheep provided wool, hides, and meat. They were easy to herd and to keep out of the crops. For most of the year they lived on the mountain slopes or out in the desert scrub. They required less grass, less water, and less care than cattle or horses.

Cattle were of some value too, but the great herds of horses were nothing but a nuisance. Horses ate the grass needed by the sheep, they were hard to manage, and just a few of them would meet all the needs of these sedentary farmers. As a result of this thinking, most of the horses were traded off to the Plains tribes, giving them more horses in a year than they could acquire in a decade of ordinary trading. This increased horse supply speeded up the spread of horses among the rest of the Plains tribes.

When the Spanish, in 1690, went to Matagorda Bay to expel the French left there by La Salle, they found a few horses near the mouth of the Colorado River of Texas, under conditions suggesting that the animals were a rather recent acquisition. Few of the Indians had horses to ride, and dogs were still used to carry the meat.[6]

[6] Herbert Eugene Bolton, *Spanish Explorations in the Southwest, 1542–1706*, p. 359.

To the north the situation was similar. Tonty, traveling south in 1690, first found horses among the Cadadoquis along the Red River near the Arkansas-Texas boundary, but only about thirty. After a few days' travel to the southwest he met the Naouadiche, who had many horses, each lodge possessing four or five.[7] This indicates that the horses were spreading from west to east in that section, and that the Cadadoquis marked the extreme limit of their advance at that time.

North of Texas there are fewer data. Tonty's report of his first trip down the Mississippi, as given by Margry,[8] indicates that he knew of horses on the Missouri River in 1682. However, his manuscript as translated by Falconer[9] does not indicate any such observation. The passage in Margry was probably written after 1695, and was based on Tonty's findings in 1690.

Horses were reported among the Pawnee, Missouri, Kansas, and Ponca by 1700, but the first eye-witness account of such horses is given by Du Tisne,[10] who found

[7] Thomas Falconer, *On the Discovery of the Mississippi, and on the South-western, Oregon, and North-western Boundary of the United States. With a Translation from the Original Manuscripts, Memoirs, etc., Relating to the Discovery of the Mississippi, by Robert Cavelier de La Salle and the Chevalier Henry de Tonty*, pp. 88–89.

[8] Pierre Margry, *Memoires et documents pour servir a l'histoire des origines francaises des pays d'outre-mer. Découvertes et établissements des Francais dans l'ouest et dans le sud de l'Amerique Septentrionale (1614–1754)*, VI, 248.

[9] Falconer, *op. cit.*, pp. 88–89.

[10] Margry, *op. cit.*, VI, 312.

YOUNG KIOWA BRAVE. Courtesy of the Marion Koogler McNay Art Institute, San Antonio, Texas.

This is one from a series of drawings in pencil and wax crayon, the work of Silver Horns, a Kiowa Indian living at Fort Sill in the Indian territory in the 1880's. Sketching materials including the oblong leather-bound album in which the drawings were made were provided him by the Indian agent at Fort Sill, but otherwise Silver Horns' work is completely free of the white man's touch. The sketchbook dates from around 1887, as attested by the inscription of the Indian interpreter at Fort Sill at this date, Howard C. Jones. Jones was fluent in both Kiowa and Comanche and gave an English title and interpretation to each sketch. The scenes depicted are those of the period fifteen to twenty years before the drawings were made, when the Kiowas were at war not only with the whites but with almost every Indian tribe whose lands were contingent to Kiowa territory. The young Kiowa warrior in the sketch illustrated rides his spotted horse to raise volunteers for a war party.

AUGUSTE AND HIS HORSE. Alfred Jacob Miller. Courtesy of the Walters Art Gallery, Baltimore, Maryland.

In 1837 Captain William Drummond Stewart, an eccentric Scot who had fought with Wellington, the heir apparent to the estates of Murthly and Grandtully in Scotland, was planning what he felt sure was his last trip to the Rocky Mountains and other parts of western North America. Following the trail blazed a few years earlier by Prince Maximilian von Wied-Nieuwied, who had commissioned Karl Bodmer to make a complete pictorial record of his travels in the American West, Stewart engaged Alfred Jacob Miller, a young Baltimore portrait painter fresh from the art academies of Paris, to perform a like service for

his farewell expedition. His travels over, the Scotsman took young Miller to Scotland to be a guest in his castle while the painter completed the large oils commissioned from the rough sketches made on the trail. In after years, back in Baltimore, Miller occasionally picked up extra money by making finished water colors or oils from his original camp sketches. This illustration is taken from the series of two hundred water colors commissioned by William T. Walters of Baltimore in 1858, now in the Museum which Walters founded. Auguste was a half-breed Canadian scout for the expedition, described by Miller as the best of all their mountain men and the life of the camp.

about three hundred horses in the Pawnee villages in Oklahoma near the Arkansas River. He found these horses valued highly, and not for sale.

Bourgmont,[11] on his trip up the Missouri River to the Plains in 1724, likewise crossed the border of the horse area. The Kansas Indians who accompanied him to the Plains did not take horses on the trip, but later Bourgmont met farther west some Kansas Indians who did have a few horses, and he managed to buy seven at a high price.

The Vérendryes,[12] who came from Canada to trade with the Mandan villages of North Dakota, found no horses owned that far north. Until 1743 the northern limit of horse using Indians was the Black Hills, as indicated in the Vérendrye journals.

This slow spread of the horse on the Plains is significant in relation to horses west of the Rocky Mountains and on their eastern slope. In 1754 Anthony Hendry,[13] an employee of Hudson's Bay Company, visited in the western Saskatchewan plains Indians who had horses. It is obvious that these Indians secured them from some western source, for their tradition is that their first horses came from the Flatheads west of the mountains. They

probably secured their first horses not later than 1745, and possibly as early as 1740. Hence the Flatheads would have had horses by 1730, securing them from the Shoshone around Three Forks, Montana.

But the Shoshone had a few horses as far north as the Canadian border in the 1730's,[14] when they used the animals in battle against the Piegan branch of the Blackfeet. If thirty years is allowed for the spread of horses from the vicinity of Pocatello, Idaho, to the Marias River in Montana, the Shoshone of the upper Snake Valley had horses by 1700 or a little earlier.

From The Dalles, Oregon, comes a story which corroborates this estimate:

> There are now old men living at the Dalles and among kindred tribes in the vicinity who say they remember seeing other old men who were living when the horse was first introduced among them. They say that the first horses obtained were looked upon as great curiosities, and as their use was not known, the animals were kept merely for show and as pets. They were led about in the festive processions, and were present at all dances and fêtes. This must have been about 125 years ago.[15]

Since this account was written in 1855, this would place the first horses at The Dalles about 1730. To pass from southeastern Idaho to The Dalles, which would take about thirty years or a little more, they would have had to come through at least two intermediaries, the Boise Valley Shoshone and either the Nez Perce or the Cayuse.

---

[11] Phil E. Chappell, "History of the Missouri River," *Kansas Historical Collections*, IX (1904–1906), 237–316, 260.

[12] Lawrence Burpee (ed.), *Journals and Letters of Pierre Gautier de Varennes de La Vérendrye and His Sons: With Correspondence between the Governors of Canada and the French Court, Touching on the Search for the Western Sea*, p. 387.

[13] Anthony Hendry, *Journal, Proceedings and Transactions*, Royal Society of Canada, 3rd Series, 1 (1907), 329–357.

[14] John Ewers, *The Horse in Blackfoot Indian Culture*, p. 17.

[15] *Pacific Railway Survey Reports*, XII, Bk. II, p. 139. Note that Ewers did not have this item.

Such an occurrence would indicate horses around Pocatello about 1700 or a little earlier. The Nez Perce tradition is that they bought their first horse from the Boise Valley Shoshone. From the above data, this could have been as early as 1720.[16]

West of the Rocky Mountains the horses moved north more rapidly than they did in the Great Plains. Here in southwestern Colorado and in Utah, the rough, arid country offered scant pasture. As each small group of Indians acquired all the horses their land could support, they were willing to trade off any surplus to their northern neighbors. In the Great Plains, where pastures extended in all directions and grass was plentiful, it required many more horses to fill each hundred miles of the area as the horses moved northward. The approximate routes of the northward movement of the horses are shown on the map on p. 69. As a result of such significantly different conditions west of the mountains, compared to the conditions east of the mountains, the horses in the west had spread to the north of the Great Salt Lake by 1690, at a time when the horse frontier east of the Rockies was still in Oklahoma.

The Snake River Valley, from American Falls east to the Continental Divide, was good horse country. In the summers the higher slopes offered cool, abundant pasture, while the many small valleys gave protection against winter storms. Springs and streams were well distributed throughout the range. When winter snows covered the rolling hills and upland meadows, the desert water holes filled, allowing the stock to pasture on the bunch grass scattered among the desert scrub.

Even with such natural advantages, the Shoshone herds increased only slowly, for interested neighbors on all sides proved ready and willing to help themselves to this new wealth. Crows from the Yellowstone, Blackfeet from Alberta, Flatheads from the Bitterroot Valley, Cayuse from the Blue Mountains, and Nez Perce from the Clearwater all looked to the Shoshone for their horses.

Horses and Culture Patterns

The basic problem of primitive man was to secure food and shelter, his culture pattern being built around his main food supply. Hence the culture of the Plains Indian was based on buffalo hunting, since the buffalo supplied him with food, clothing, shelter, tools, and fuel. For centuries the buffalo-hunting tribes had been seminomadic, following the buffalo herds as best they could for a large part of the year.[17]

All their possessions had to be transported on the backs of dogs or humans, thus limiting them to the bare essentials. Their shelters were small, light tipis of buffalo hide

---

[16] Herbert J. Spinden, "Nez Perce Tales," *Journal of American Folk-lore*, XXI (1908), 158.

[17] Robert H. Lowie, *Indians of the Plains*, pp. 13–16.

and sticks, their weapons few, and their food stock scanty. Only when a buffalo herd could be driven into snowdrifts or onto smooth ice in the winter, or over a cliff in the summer, could they be free, even for a short time, from the threat of famine.

During the summer months, when the buffalo were hardest to kill, the Indians stayed along the little water courses, raising small patches of corn, beans, and squash. These, with wild berries and some small game, tided them over the lean months, but always they were dependent on the buffalo herds for most of their living. Their great problem was to develop some means of following the buffalo herds more closely so they could kill the animals at more regular intervals throughout the year.

The horse furnished the obvious answer to this problem, and could be used by the Indians with no change in their basic culture pattern. With horses, they could follow the buffalo herds more closely, and could kill almost any number of animals they chose. Surplus meat from large kills, dried or in pemmican, could be carried on the pack horses. More buffalo robes and larger tipis were now easy to procure and to transport.

Even so, the process of adapting a tribe to the full use of horses required many years. The older men could see the advantage of using horses in place of dogs to carry the packs, but they refused to learn to ride, preferring to trudge along on foot, leading the pack animals, while the younger men dashed about on horseback. In each band the daring, reckless, younger men were the first to learn to ride. Once they learned, their younger brothers had to learn, as a new test of manhood. Not until the passing years had placed these horsemen in positions of power and influence in the tribe was tribal life really adjusted to the new conditions. The process from the acquisition of the first horses until the tribe had fully adopted them required in each case about twenty years.

In the Columbia Basin the culture pattern was based on salmon fishing. The villages were small permanent settlements near the good fishing places. Some of the fishermen built large houses, using heavy logs and planks. The main travel routes were along the rivers, from one village to another, with dugout canoes in common use.

For a fishing tribe to make effective use of horses it would have to make drastic changes in its way of living and its general culture pattern. Seldom would good pasture for horses be found near a good fishing place. Any travel with horses in the Columbia Basin would follow the higher ground, away from the rivers which usually flow in deep, narrow valleys or canyons. To many of the fishing tribes, therefore, the horse would be more of an expensive luxury than a benefit. It comes as something of a surprise, then, to learn that the two Indian tribes most famous for their horses in all North America were two of the salmon-fishing tribes of the Columbia Basin. They were the Cayuse, who gave their name to the

NEZ PERCE INDIANS, *ca.* 1895. Photograph courtesy Mary Himes, Cayuse, Oregon.

On the basis of the dress of the two Indians and the style of the saddle on the well-marked Appaloosa in the background this picture would indicate a date in the late nineteenth century. The Indian on the left is a son of the Indian Poker Jim of the western band of Nez Perce, often called the Palouse Indians.

This picture is made available by Mary Himes, who remembers the Indian on the left. Because the Indians on the Lapwai Reservation were under the control of the missionaries there were few Appaloosa horses among them, this horse having been a symbol of the warlike tendencies of the rebellious Nez Perce. For this reason it is thought that this early photograph was probably taken on either the Umatilla or the Nespeolem Reservation.

OGLALA SIOUX TIPI LINING. Courtesy of the Museum of the American Indian, Heye Foundation, New York City.

Painted on muslin, this cloth is one-half of a once complete section of a lining used inside the poles of a tipi, thus providing insulation against cold and moisture. This example was collected by E. W. Lenders, nineteenth-century artist traveling in the upper Missouri Valley. His records indicate that this example was secured at Pine Ridge, South Dakota, about 1890 and was drawn by an Oglala Sioux man who told Lenders that the drawing (the complete drawing is not recorded) was an account of his war exploits up to the time of Wounded Knee. Unfortunately Lenders did not record the events or if he did they did not accompany his collection of objects.

The episodes recorded include ceremonies, buffalo and deer hunting, and war parties. The central figure, wearing a horned mask and carrying a painted shield, is mounted on a blanket-type Appaloosa.

western-range horse, and the Nez Perce, who bred the Appaloosas.

Nez Perce Stockmen[18]

It happened that the Nez Perce and the Cayuse lived in country even better suited to horse raising than the Shoshone area in southeastern Idaho, and much better protected against enemy raids. Perhaps the combination of excellent stock country and rather mediocre fishing places set them on the new road that changed them from sedentary fishing tribes to seminomadic hunting tribes. Perhaps their practice, developed through necessity, of supplementing their fish diet with various berries, roots, and game animals made them more sturdy and progressive, more willing to try new ways. Whatever the cause, the Cayuse and the Nez Perce made rapid progress in horse raising.

Deep, sheltered valleys, about a thousand feet above sea level, and protected from blizzards by the mountain rampart to the east, furnished winter pasture. In summer the herds found ample forage and pleasant weather on the plateau, two to three thousand feet higher than the valley floors, and but a few miles away. The protecting mountains barred enemy horse thieves as effectually as they warded off winter storms. Wolves and mountain lions were scarce.

The Nez Perce, almost from the first, practiced some selective breeding. Their methods, however, could not compare with the elaborate programs of today. They consisted chiefly of castrating some of the poorer stallions[19] and of disposing of poorer stock to the neighbors. At any rate, their breeding was effective, for the Nez Perce produced better horses than other tribes did, and some of the tribes rated Nez Perce horses above those stolen from the Spanish ranches. Here is an evaluation by one of the first white men to visit the tribe, Meriwether Lewis, who was a skilled horseman from Virginia, in an extract from his daily journal, dated Saturday, February 15, 1806:

Their horses appear to be of an excellent race; they are lofty, eligantly [sic] formed, active and durable; in short many of them look like fine English coarsers [sic] and would make a figure in any country. *Some of those horses are pided with large spots of white irregularly scattered and intermixed with the black, brown, bey or some other dark color* [italics added]; but much the larger portion are of a uniform color with stars, snips, and white feet, or in this rispect [sic] marked much like our best blooded horses in Virginia, which they resemble as well in fleetness and bottom as in form and color.[20]

Lewis also gives an account of the Nez Perce method of gelding animals, which followed the Spanish practice. This makes it probable that the Nez Perce learned their gelding method from an Indian from the Spanish settle-

---

[18] Francis Haines, *The Nez Perces: Tribesmen of the Columbia Plateau*, pp. 3–310. This contains the Nez Perce story in detail, and has a comprehensive bibliography of pertinent materials.

[19] Reuben Gold Thwaites (ed.), *The Original Journals of the Lewis and Clark Expedition, 1804–1806*, VI, 36, 39, 58–59.

[20] *Ibid.*, IV, Pt. 1, 73.

PANCHO A IN A STAKE RACE. Courtesy of Jim and Jean Atkinson, Kenedy, Texas.

Nez Perce Stake Race. The Nez Perce were fond of all types of horse racing. Some of their races involved weaving through natural barriers or racing to a certain rock or tree, turning around it and returning. Many of the races involved only two horses. The Nez Perce Stake Race is run through poles, horse against horse (rather than against a stop watch) until the elimination is complete. The winning horse often has run as many as eight races before the elimination is complete.

ments. Even so, their adoption of this practice under the circumstances is probably unique in the history of primitive people. The account by Lewis, quoted above, not only stresses the quality of the Nez Perce herds in 1806, but also shows that the tribe had Appaloosas at that time. The italicized material above could not apply to a paint, pinto, or calico-marked horse.

As the herds of fine horses increased on the Nez Perce pastures, the tribe became skilled in horsemanship and adapted their new servants to many uses. The hunters rode to the plateau after antelope, or to the mountains for deer, bear, elk, and mountain sheep. Family groups traveled to the camas meadows and to the berry patches. More intervillage and intertribal visiting was done, with various leaders meeting to discuss common problems in great intertribal councils.

The common horses were traded in large numbers to other tribes when the Nez Perce wanted to buy anything. At The Dalles, dried salmon, sea shells, and other products of the coast tribes were taken in exchange. Crows from the Yellowstone offered buffalo robes, bright with quill work. Pipestone from the Minnesota quarries, buffalo-horn spoons, Sioux war bonnets, and other handicraft of the Great Plains were traded west across the mountains to the Nez Perce, who thus served as a connecting link on trade routes that reached from the Pacific to the coast of New England.

Once the Nez Perce became expert horsemen they began to cross the mountains to the buffalo country.

With their superior horses they had little difficulty in killing what buffalo they needed. They brought back large stores of tanned buffalo robes and dried meat. Soon they began to use the Plains-type tipi in place of their old community houses with the massive timber framework and the covering of tule mats. Heavy stone mortars and similar burdensome possessions were either discarded entirely, or were left at the fishing spots for occasional use.

The Nez Perce bow became famous among the buffalo hunters. Sometimes it was made of fine cedar backed with layers of sinew held in place with fish glue. A better bow was made of strips of horn from mountain sheep, similarly reinforced.[21] Such a bow was short enough to carry on horseback, and powerful enough to drive an arrow through the paunch of a buffalo. Several cases were recorded in which calves running close to their mothers' flanks were killed by the same arrow that slew the parent. Nez Perce bows were always in demand, a good bow being valued at the price of a good horse.

Under the impact of the new horse culture the Nez Perce tribe split into two groups. The larger portion, in less than a century, had changed their culture from that of fishermen living in small, permanent villages along the western rivers, to that of seminomadic bands roaming from the mouth of the Snake River in Washington to the plains of central Montana, and depending largely

[21] Marvin C. Ross, *The West of Alfred Jacob Miller*, opposite Plate 7. Shows a good picture of the Nez Perce compound bow.

BRANDING ON THE OPEN RANGE near Burns, Oregon. Photograph by Henry H. Sheldon, Portland, Oregon.

One roper has "headed" the calf, the other has "heeled" it. Both men are dally ropers. The horses maintain the correct tension on the ropes, enough to hold the calf steady for branding, yet not enough to injure it.

JOKER B. Courtesy of the Cee Bar Ranch, Celina, Texas.

Steer roping requires not only speed, but the strength, ruggedness, and power to stop the weight and drive of the steer. Appa-loosas have the "will to work" that is required of a horse handling heavy stock.

on buffalo for their living. They borrowed so many culture traits from the various Plains tribes that it is difficult to determine exactly what their culture might have been before the coming of the horse.

During this period of great change, ca. 1790–1810, a conservative minority refused to accept the new ways. They preferred to live in their little villages, and shunned the long, hard trip across the mountains to the buffalo land. At home they were safe from attack, but on the Plains they were always in danger from the Blackfeet. However the two groups remained friendly, the split often coming within a family.

All the western tribes feared the Blackfeet, who were brave, hardy, and numerous. Hudson's Bay Company traders had brought guns to them early in the eighteenth century, giving them a great advantage in war over their neighbors. Blackfeet war parties, in addition to being well armed, were large, often numbering a thousand men. Other tribes considered a war party of two hundred large. Also the Blackfeet, unlike the other tribes, waged wars of extermination against their enemies in order to occupy more land.

When the Nez Perce invaded the buffalo country claimed by the Blackfeet, they had to rely on extra vigilance to discover their danger in time, and on the speed of their horses to carry them to safety. Not until they secured plenty of guns were they able to fight the Blackfeet on equal terms.

War Horses and Buffalo Hunters

Even among the Nez Perce herds, built up by some selective breeding, not all the horses were fast. Many of them were mediocre animals—scrubs, culls, and worn-out pack animals—kept for trading purposes. Next to these in value were the group used as pack horses and as mounts for women and old people. They were usually gentle, well-broken animals of mediocre ability. These groups made up the majority of any horse herd.

All the better horses, much fewer in number, were reserved for the men. These included many sound, easy-gaited animals for ordinary traveling. Such horses need not be showy or especially speedy. Above them were the aristocrats of the herds, the buffalo hunters and the war horses. To be included in this select group, a horse had to

be able to give a buffalo a quarter-mile head start and overtake the frightened animal in less than two miles. Buffalo hunters had to be trained much like our stock horses, so they would do their work without much attention from their riders, who were busy with their weapons. The horse was expected to follow any animal selected by the rider, and to approach so closely that the rider could touch the animal with his foot. Such well-trained, speedy horses were carefully guarded, and were not for sale.

Of course speedy buffalo hunters came in all colors, many of them appearing drab to the Indians. For special occasions this unattractive aspect could be remedied by decorating such horses with feathers, ribbons, and splashes of paint. In time of battle—if there was time—horses were always decorated. Some of the horses had natural-color patterns which made them look gaudy alongside the solid-color animals. If they were speedy, too, they were especially prized, for they made ideal war horses. Even in a surprise attack the horse was ready, and the sweat of battle could not make his colors run or blur. For this reason some of the Plains tribes valued fleet pintos above all others. Such horses attracted the eye of any artist who saw the mounted Indians, with the result that pintos are prominent in frontier art. Many people today consider the pinto the typical Indian horse, because they have seen it pictured so often.

The Nez Perce, however, did not commonly ride the

CALF ROPING, Joseph, Oregon. Picture courtesy Appaloosa Horse Club.

    Roping on the open range is far more difficult than under the specialized conditions seen in the rodeo ring. The horse, as always, has to play his part by holding the rope tight on the calf until the animal has been tied. Appaloosa horses are seen as often on the working range as in the dude-ranch strings.

pinto, probably because they had a better horse with a color pattern at least as striking. This was the horse with the spotted white rump, the Appaloosa, whose ancestors we have been tracing through twenty thousand years. The Nez Perce claimed that these animals were doubly advantageous: they were speedy, tough, intelligent, and hardy; they were perfectly colored to look flashy at close range, but because of the spotted coat which blended at a distance with the background in a natural camouflage, to be especially valuable in enemy country.

In the light of this evidence, it is quite possible that some of the earliest horses in the Nez Perce country were spotted, and came up through the Great Basin from the New Mexico ranches. Even a few well-spotted horses in the Nez Perce country could multiply into many in a hundred years, especially since these Indians did some selective breeding. "Colonel" Rogers, of Grangeville, Idaho, who saw the herd of the Wallowa band, estimated that by the time of the Nez Perce War in 1877 from a third to a half of their horses consisted of spotted stock.

Le Bleu of Spokane House

Beyond the Rocky Mountains, if these should be passed, a still nobler instance of animal production will be found. The horse of the Columbia River, taken all in all, is perhaps the finest animal of his kind in the known world. He is derived from the old world, but instead of degenerating, has improved on the banks of the Columbia. Fineness of form, fulness of all muscular parts, docility of spirit, capacity to sustain great fatigue, to provide food for himself, and to hunt down the deer and the buffalo for his master, are a part of his characteristics . . .[22]

In the river bottom, near the confluence of the Spokane and Little Spokane rivers, John Jacob Astor's men built a trading post, Spokane House, designed to draw trade from the rival Northwest Company post, Fort Spokane. For two years a bitter trade rivalry existed between the two posts.

Spokane House soon developed into a social center, with many dances and parties during the winter to entertain the traders and their Indian friends. In the summer the chief sport was horse racing, which attracted large crowds of participants and spectators. Pride of the Spokane House stables was Le Bleu, described as "dappled white and skyblue." He was somewhat larger than the usual Indian horse of his day, measuring fifteen hands, two inches, at the withers. At the age of seven he had beaten all the best horses in the Spokane House races for two seasons.

One summer morning the Spokane House factor, John Clarke, received an emergency message from a party of his men in the Flathead country to the east. A large party of Indians, with plenty of fur to trade, had just arrived and was camped between Clarke's men and a party of Northwesters. The Indians refused to trade with either group until they had been given their customary treat of smoking tobacco. Both groups of traders

[22] *Niles Weekly Register*, XVI, No. 23 (July 31, 1819), 377.

CROW INDIAN PAINTING ON ELK SKIN. Courtesy of the Museum of the American Indian, Heye Foundation, New York City.

Collected from a Crow Indian family near Browning, Montana, by the late Dr. George G. Heye about 1910. The painting was made *ca.* 1895. The artist shows an incident during a buffalo hunt which is being shared by both Indian braves mounted and on foot and by three presumably white men dressed as cowboys of that day. The white men ride pinto horses while all but one of the Indians are mounted on Appaloosas.

were entirely out of tobacco, and the whole supply of furs would go to those who could first secure the much desired stuff for smoking. A messenger from the camp had reached Fort Spokane just as Clarke's man reached Spokane House.

Immediately both posts were in a turmoil, saddling horses, packing tobacco, and preparing riders. Clarke chose one of his smaller men, Ross Cox, and mounted him on Le Bleu. Here is Cox's story of the ride:

Owing to the delay occasioned by catching the horses we did not start till twelve o'clock. I remained in company with the men [his two companions] for the first two hours at a slight canter, after which I took the lead in a hard gallop, and quickly lost sight of them. I followed an excellent well-beaten pathway for upwards of sixty miles through the Pointed Heart Plains [Coeur d'Alene]; but late in the evening brought me to a thick wood, through which it runs for a distance of ten miles, when it terminates at the portage.

Shortly after entering the wood, night overtook me; and I several times lost the pathway, which, owing to darkness, and a quantity of fallen trees and brushwood, became extremely intricate. The sagacity of my horse, however, extricated me from these *egaremens*, and a little after eight o'clock I emerged from the forest, and was delighted at the appearance of a range of fires along the banks of the river. The Bleu, which had been for some time drooping, on seeing the light, knew his task was at an end, and galloped up in fine style to Farnham's tent, when he was immediately let loose to regale himself.[23]

So Le Bleu brought the good news and the tobacco,

and the furs went to Clarke's men, for the competitors did not arrive until two hours later.

We returned to Spokane House by easy stages; but I did not ride the Bleu. In less than a week after he was perfectly recovered from his journey, and in the summer of the same year beat the fleetest horses of both Companies, on the race-course.

Missionary Influence on the Nez Perce

The Lewis and Clark Expedition brought the first white men into the Nez Perce country, and introduced the tribe to some of the products of civilization. The explorers were followed in turn by Astor's men, the Northwesters, and Hudson's Bay Company employees. Those traders and trappers, with their superior tools, weapons, and other mechanical contrivances, convinced the Nez Perce that the white men possessed some sort of spiritual helpers stronger than those of the Indians. In some way the Nez Perce came to believe that they must learn to read and write if they wished to secure spiritual aid from the same source.

This desire for white man's learning led the tribe to send a delegation to St. Louis in 1831 asking for teachers. Soon several missionaries were sent to the Columbia Basin in answer to this request. Two of them, Henry Harmon Spalding and his wife Eliza, settled among the Nez Perce at Lapwai in 1836.[24]

[23] Ross Cox, *The Columbia River*, pp. 245–246.

[24] E. M. Drury, *Henry Harmon Spalding*, pp. 17–417.

CUTTING HORSE. Photograph by Miehle Studios, Riverside, California.

A good cutting horse does his own thinking. He learns from the way a cow acts what to expect her to do and what he must do to stop her. Appaloosas have a reputation for having natural "cow sense" plus the agility to cut cattle smoothly and efficiently. Being widely used on cattle ranches throughout the Northwest for the past one hundred years, Appaloosas are considered the world's best rough-country cow horse.

CUTTING HORSE, Wynnewood, Oklahoma. Courtesy Beau Cheval Ranch. Picture by John Williams, Ardmore, Oklahoma.

While the Appaloosa is popular for his unique coat, he is also a fine working horse. Cutting out calves is a tricky chore requiring instant reflexes and speed. A good cutting horse can do the job virtually without a rider.

MARES AND COLT on George Hatley ranch, Moscow, Idaho. From the film "The Appaloosa Horse," Fred Rice Productions, Van Nuys, California.

The Spaldings were successful from the first. In a short time they had taught several hundred Indians to read, and to write a little, in their own language. A church was organized, with a large group in attendance each Sunday. Indian families settled near the mission and learned to tend gardens and to raise grain, sheep, and hogs. Under the influence of the missionaries many of the families gave up many of their old customs and practices, such as racing horses, hunting buffalo, and fighting Blackfeet.

From the first, the more conservative portion of the tribe supplied most of the converts. They liked to stay in their little villages, depending on the salmon and camas for their principal foods instead of traveling the long, dangerous road to the buffalo country and fighting with the fierce tribes there. Farming and stock tending fitted into their scheme of living and they soon, under the white man's supervision, became fairly successful farmers.

Adventurous young men who liked to race horses, to gamble, and to go on the warpath poked fun at the stay-at-homes. They would ride by the garden patches on hot summer days and invite their farmer friends to quit their squaw work. Why not drop their hoes, catch their best horses, and join them on a pleasure jaunt? Often the farmers would do so, to the great annoyance of Henry Spalding.

The missionaries believed that their converts would become better Christians and better farmers if they gave up their native culture and became more like eastern farmers. Native dress, feasts, gambling games, council meetings, and pleasure trips might lead the Indians into bad company and hinder their adoption of the white man's ways.[25] Fast spotted horses were particularly bad, for they might encourage their owners to go to war, or to enter races, and thus lead church members into sin.

Thus it happened that the more independent members of the tribe continued to breed and raise fast Appaloosas for use in the buffalo country while their farmer brethren raised solid-color work horses. So firmly was the idea implanted that fast Appaloosas, and, incidentally, native dress, were only for heathen Indians that even now, more than a century later, some of the good church members among the Nez Perce would not care to own an Appaloosa horse, or to dress in Indian costume for a parade.

After the Spaldings had worked at Lapwai for about eleven years, the neighboring Cayuse Indians at Walla Walla killed their missionary, Dr. Marcus Whitman, along with his wife, Narcissa, and twelve of the men at the mission. The resulting unrest and disorders caused the Spaldings to abandon their mission station. The Nez Perce were then left to their own devices for several years.

[25] Indian Agency Correspondence, Lapwai, Idaho, January 1, 1871–December 31, 1876 (Idaho Historical Library, Boise, Idaho). Especially letters of John Monteith, Indian Agent, Lapwai, Idaho, to Indian Bureau, Washington, D. C.

BARREL RACE. Photograph by Jim Mischel, Ephrata, Washington.

Appaloosas are popular for barrel racing. Barrel racing requires a series of bursts of speed and fast turns. The state champion in open, all-breed competition for the State of Washington in 1960 was an Appaloosa.

How the Appaloosa Became a Lost Breed

In 1860 the discovery of rich placer diggings on the Nez Perce reservation brought thousands of settlers. They took most of the tribal lands which the United States government had guaranteed to the tribe under the treaty of 1855, and were angry because they could not take more. To further complicate matters about half the tribe rejected the new treaty and were then known as the "nontreaty" bands.

By 1870 homesteaders had settled along much of the reservation boundary. They liked to pasture their stock on the unfenced range, largely reservation land. Soon they were complaining that the Indian horses were eating all the grass on the ranges, ignoring the fact that the grass belonged to the Indians, confirmed to them by two solemn treaties. The settlers complained, too, of Indian stallions on the range. They did not want their heavy-boned, plodding farm horses crossed with such stock. They believed that the trim, hardy Indian horses must be of poor quality because they were smaller, and had too much spirit.

About this time the reservation was put in charge of a man selected by the Presbyterian Board, but hired by the Indian Bureau. This new agent, John Monteith, followed much the same program Spalding had instituted among the Nez Perce some thirty-five years earlier. He, too, disapproved of the Indians' raising riding horses.[26] Such

26 *Ibid.*

APPALOOSA AT CHARRO CLUB, MEXICO, D.F.
Courtesy Dick Spencer, III, Editor, *The Western Horseman,* Colorado Springs, Colorado.

horses could be sold at fair prices to the towns and mining camps, giving the breeders more ready money than they could make by any other sort of work. With ready money to spend for supplies they were less dependent on the agent and his distribution of the treaty payments. If the agent's regulations became too burdensome, or if he became too dictatorial, these Indians could pack their things and go to the buffalo country for a year or two, thus escaping all supervision.

Finally, Monteith secured permission to use the army to force all the nontreaty bands onto the reservation. The richest and largest of these was the Wallowa band led by their young chief, Joseph. They pastured several thousand head of horses and cattle between the Wallowa Mountains and the Snake River Canyon in northeastern Oregon.

Under threat of attack by the cavalry, the Joseph band began a hurried roundup of their stock and moved with all their families, possessions, and herds into the Snake River Canyon. Here they swam the roaring torrent in full flood. They lost about nine hundred animals, but the people were safe.

As they camped on Camas Prairie between Cottonwood and Grangeville, Idaho, with other nontreaty bands, a fifteen-year-old boy from Grangeville rode out near the camp. In 1948 he recalled vividly the plain covered with spotted horses, but a closer look revealed there were about an equal number of plain animals mixed with the spotted ones.[27]

[27] The author is indebted to "Colonel" Rogers, long time resident of Grangeville, Idaho, whose eye-witness reports of the Nez Perce herds have been used in their narrative. Rogers was later dispatch rider for General O. O. Howard during the Nez Perce campaign.

Three young men from the Salmon River band went out for private revenge and killed four settlers. This sparked a raid by twenty more warriors, and the war was on. Captain Perry set out from Fort Lapwai with two companies of cavalry to attack the Indian camp. After a forced march of about ninety miles they found the Nez Perce shortly after sunrise on June 17 on White Bird Creek. The Indians had about 65 men to oppose Captain Perry's 112, but in a few minutes the soldiers had been defeated with a loss of 34 killed, 2 soldiers and 2 civilians wounded. The Indians had 2 wounded. Now followed a game of hide-and-seek for three and a half months—the Nez Perce bands with all their families being chased by a total of five more armies.

General Howard, the Department commander, with 580 men made a surprise attack on the Nez Perce camp on the South Fork of the Clearwater. Here the Nez Perce could muster about a hundred men, but they fought Howard to a draw on July 11 and 12; then they retreated across 150 miles of rough mountains to the Bitterroot Valley of Montana, where they outwitted Captain Rawn with a small force and moved south across the Continental Divide to a camp on the Big Hole River.

BUFFALO BILL. by Rosa Bonheur. Courtesy of the Whitney Gallery of Western Art, Cody, Wyoming.

Rosa Bonheur made a name for herself as the leading painter of horses in France in the late nineteenth century, when women were not expected to be professional painters, much less to paint horses. William Cody, the American cavalry scout-buffalo hunter turned theatrical entrepreneur, rode a horse so well that an observer with a classical background pronounced him the closest thing to a centaur possible in nature. When Buffalo Bill's Wild West Show reached Paris during its tour of the continent in 1889 a meeting between the horse painter and the horse rider was inevitable. Rosa spent many hours in the backyard of the Show, painting the innumerable varieties of horses assembled from all over the world for the Cossacks, gauchos, and cowboys in the show to ride. Among the paintings she executed at this time is the portrait of Buffalo Bill riding his favorite mount, a spotted horse variously identified as "Sultan" or "Ivan". Cody had a showman's appreciation for the decorative appeal of the Appaloosa, and used them frequently in his Shows.

Rosa Bonheur
— 1889 —

MALIBU CHIEF JUMPING. Photograph by R. S. Draughon, Baton Rouge, Louisiana.
Appaloosas have the courage and the ability to perform well as hunters and jumpers. This horse
is winning the Hunter Class at the National Appaloosa Show.

At this spot they were surprised in their beds by Colonel Gibbon, with 192 men, and lost 89 killed. Managing to beat Gibbon off, they went southwest across the Divide into southern Idaho and then swung east. Here they stole pack mules from Howard's pursuing army and retreated across Yellowstone Park and northern Wyoming, another rugged mountain area. When their old friends, the Crows, refused them sanctuary, they turned north across Montana and planned to join the Sioux under Sitting Bull in Canada.

They were trapped by the new telegraph line into Fort Keogh. Thanks to this recently strung wire, General Howard was able to send word to Colonel Miles, who took his troops and raced north and then west across the

ROY LAFOLLETTE ON APPALOOSA. Photograph courtesy of Nell P. Lafollette, Moscow, Idaho.

This picture of Roy Lafollette was taken about 1908. The date is approximate and based on the style of chaps and gauntlets which were then in common use by Western horsemen.

Montana plains to intercept the fugitives, watchful of their back trail to the south but ignorant of this new danger now approaching from the east.

Once again, while preparing to break camp on the morning of September 29, 1877, the Nez Perce suffered a surprise attack. Colonel Miles attempted to wipe them out in a single charge, for he had nearly 600 men to oppose 120 Nez Perce, and he had the advantage of surprise. His charge was stopped short of the camp.

Then followed six days of siege. When General Howard arrived with reinforcements, the Nez Perce surrendered. Only two of their chiefs were still alive, Joseph and White Bird, who escaped to Canada. Most of the fighting men were gone. This left Joseph to conduct the surrender, a task which he performed with great dignity. The Secretary of War thus reported the occasion:

Then old Captain John brought this reply (and his lips quivered and his eyes filled with tears as he delivered the words of his chief):

"Tell General Howard I know his heart. What he told me before, I have in my heart. I am tired of fighting. Our chiefs are killed. Looking Glass is dead. Toohoolhoolzote is dead. The old men are all dead. It is the young men who say yes and no. He who led on the young men is dead. It is cold and we have no blankets. The little children are freezing to death. My people, some of them, have run away to the hills and have no blankets, no food; no one knows where they are—perhaps freezing to death. I want to have time to look for my children and see how many I can find. Maybe I shall find them among the dead. Hear me, my chiefs. I am tired; my heart is sick and sad. From where the sun now stands I will fight no more forever."[28]

Two hours later, Joseph rode slowly up the hill, accompanied by five of his warriors on foot. When he reached the group of waiting officers, he dismounted and, with an impulsive gesture, offered his rifle to Howard in token of surrender. Howard stepped back and indicated with his hand that Miles should receive it. The chief was then put under guard.

Among other items, the Nez Perce surrendered 1,100 horses. These were the toughest, hardiest animals. Most of them had lasted through the entire war and had covered thirteen hundred miles of rough country in three and a half months. They included the survivors of spotted-horse herds of the Joseph band. All these captured horses were taken to Fort Keogh and sold to horse buyers from the East.

Since the outbreak of the war caught the Nez Perce leaders by surprise, many of their horses were still on the open range when fighting broke out. A large number escaped the hasty roundup and were claimed later by the first white men who could corral them. They were then sold to cattlemen throughout the West, many of them in California and Oregon. This procedure of selling the range horses was encouraged by the agent and the church people on the reservation as part of the program to outlaw war horses, long hair, and tribal costumes. As a result of the war and the subsequent raiding of the ranges, the Appaloosa became a "lost" breed, its glorious history neglected until 1937.

[28] *Report of the Secretary of War*, 1877, p. 632.

AFTER THE NEZ PERCE WAR had dispersed the Indian herds, stockmen on many western ranches still raised a few Appaloosas for their own use. They liked the spotted horses for working cattle and for all the many chores a mounted man must perform around the stock. In time some of the Appaloosas attracted the attention of the circus people, who bought them to use in the big shows.

As early as 1840 a spotted horse had appeared at the Bowery Amphitheatre in New York. This highly trained horse was such an attraction that he appeared in a Currier and Ives print. It is probable that other Appaloosas were used in circus acts. The public attitude toward spotted horses is indicated in this story told by a former governor of Texas:

While I was on this canvass [1856] the Palestine *Advocate* got off this yarn on me: "There is a good joke told on **Frank Lub-**bock, our worthy Lieutenant-Governor. He has lately purchased two fine but fancy horses of the calico stripe, and as he came up from Houston he was taken for a bill sticker for a circus, and all the little boys were asking him when the circus would be along, and whether his circus had any animals. He gave them the necessary information, and report says, promised them all free tickets."

I did drive a pair of spanking spotted horses on this canvass, and who could blame the little fellows for taking me for the advance agent of a circus?[1]

The circus demand for well-marked Appaloosas raised the prices in Oregon. About 1870 the husband of Abigail Scott Duniway was buying up spotted horses at premium prices. From his stock he sorted out matched pairs and

[1] Francis Richard Lubbock, *Six Decades in Texas or Memoirs of Francis Richard Lubbock, Governor of Texas in War-time, 1861–1863*, p. 251.

ROMAN STANDING ACT, Al G. Barnes Wild Animal Circus, *ca.* 1914. Courtesy of the Hertzberg Circus Collection, San Antonio Public Library, San Antonio, Texas.

The Barnes Circus was famed for its Liberty Horse act, which featured twelve Appaloosas. Liberty Horses were frequently used in other acts, such as tandem driving, manege (dressage), and Roman standing. This trio prepares to enter Big Top using Appaloosas for Roman standing in a performance of the Al G. Barnes Circus. The equestrienne on the left is probably Alma Taylor, long-time capable performer in this circus.

sold them for $3,000 or more. He was careful to keep his selling prices secret, for his premium prices to the ranchers and Indians seldom reached $100 a head.

Then the Wild West shows, with their cowboys and Indians riding Western horses, appeared on the American scene. Buffalo Bill's Wild West Show was the most famous of these, headed by William P. Cody himself. On his European tour with his show Cody presumably met Rosa Bonheur, the French woman famous for her paintings of animals. At any rate a painting by Mme. Bonheur showing Bill Cody on an Appaloosa horse is in the collection of the Whitney Museum of Western Art, Cody, Wyoming. In addition to his spotted riding horse Cody owned a matched pair, white with black spots, which Mrs. Cody drove to a carriage.

Then the Western roundups and rodeos introduced Western horses, including Appaloosas, to the crowds. Here the flashy coats of the spotted horses attracted much attention. About the same time Charles M. Russell painted pictures with Appaloosas in the scene. He put a story in his book, *Trails Plowed Under*, which made mention of a Nez Perce on a leg-weary Appaloosa. This came to the attention of the author in early 1937 and set off the chain of events which led to this exhibition of Appaloosas in art.

In the January, 1937, *Western Horseman* the author published an article entitled "The Appaloosa, or Palouse Horse." Fan mail indicated a widespread interest in this kind of horse; so other articles followed. The result of this publicity was the incorporation of the Appaloosa Horse Club in December, 1938, with six charter members. Claude Thompson, of Moro, Oregon, was the leader and the first president.

The Appaloosa Horse Club was organized with the following objectives: to collect records and historical data relating to the origin of the Appaloosa horse; to file records and issue certificates of registration for animals thought to be fit foundation stock of the breed; to preserve, improve, and standardize the breed of spotted horses known in the Pacific Northwest as Appaloosas.

Through World War II the Appaloosa Horse Club barely stayed alive. In September, 1947, club headquarters was moved to Moscow, Idaho, and George Hatley became secretary. An American airman sent in a small snapshot from Tibet showing a spotted horse there, and the Club historian soon found the trail of the spotted horse in ancient Chinese art.

The knowledge that the Appaloosa was a horse with a historic background in the old world, and not just an Indian pony, interested many new people. The first all-Appaloosa horse show in history, at Lewiston, Idaho, in 1948, brought in new members and new horses. By 1950 the Club had grown to the point where it could successfully petition the National Association of Stallion Registration Boards for recognition.

Up to this point the Club had been accepting mem-

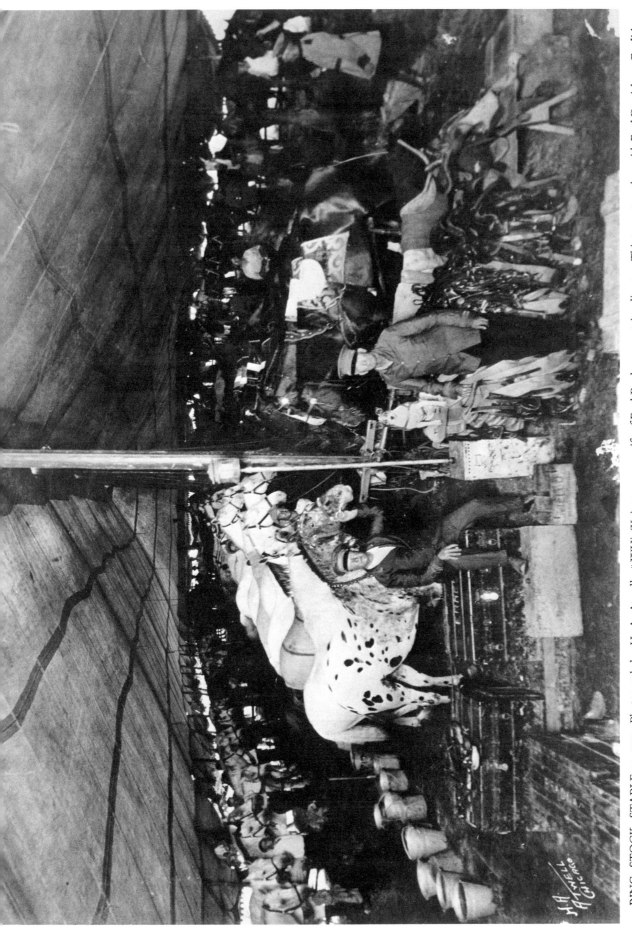

RING STOCK STABLE *ca.* 1912. Photograph by H. A. Atwell, #WHi (X3) 12032. Courtesy of the Iconographic Archives, the State Historical Society of Wisconsin, Madison. According to circus custom the most important horses in the ring stock were stabled at the entrance of the tent. The Appaloosa held by the ring stock boss wears a string of bells, which indicates that the animal was used in a bareback act. Notice the tack trunk in the foreground with the name "Bradna." This is the property of the famed Ella Bradna, equestrienne and wife of Fred Bradna, equestrian director. This team, together with Fred Derrick, an English equestrian, were aristocrats of the circus world, touring the country with Barnum & Bailey and later with Ringling Brothers. Notice the carbide lantern standing between the hostlers. This portable light, operating on gas generated by carbide and water, helps to date this photograph as prior to World War I.

bers from any country, including Canada, Great Britain, Italy, and Australia. Then both Canada and England formed horse clubs of their own. Membership in the original Club grew to the point where affiliated regional clubs were necessary, and about thirty of these are now in operation. Club membership is well over 3,000, and horse registration is over 25,000 and increasing at the rate of about 7,000 a year.

The 1963 exhibition at the Amon Carter Museum of Western Art marks an important milestone in the development of the Appaloosa and in the writing of the history of this colorful animal. It will stimulate further study and inquiry, which will in turn benefit both the horses and their owners. This summary, then, is not the end of the record. It is a progress report.

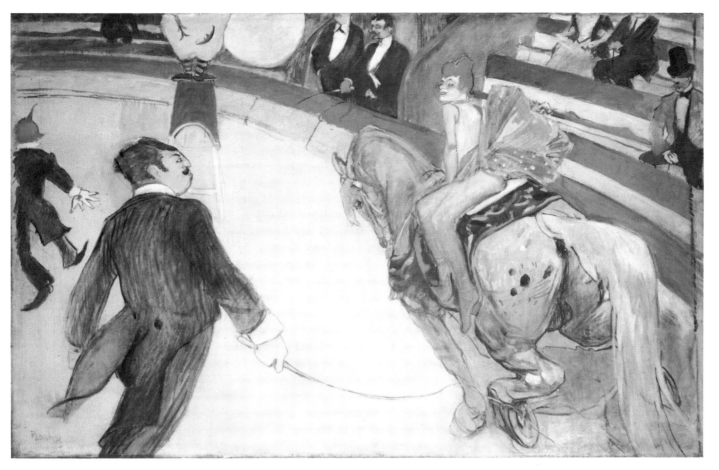

IN THE CIRCUS FERNANDO: THE RINGMASTER. Henri de Toulouse-Lautrec. Courtesy of the Art Institute of Chicago, the Joseph Winterbotham Collection, Chicago, Illinois.

At the peak of its popularity the Cirque Fernando drew the most fashionable and sophisticated Parisians to its wooden building at 63 Boulevard de Rochechouart. Artists came too, attracted by the light and color of the circus and its performers, among them the leaders of the new movements in art of the day—Renoir, Degas, and Seurat. Henri de Toulouse-Lautrec was another artist who came to paint the Cirque Fernando, especially its superb horses. From childhood Toulouse-Lautrec had loved horses and had made them the subject of numerous paintings and drawings. Strong rhythmic lines and an unrealistic perspective in this painting give the sweep of movement as the horse, its rider balanced on its back, rounds the ring under the direction of M. Loyal the Ringmaster.

Circus horses of this type, an outcross of the spotted horse and the draft horse, produce a large colorful animal ideal for bareback performances. Today the European circuses abound in dramatically marked horses for equestrian and Liberty acts.

BIBLIOGRAPHY

Anderson, J. K. *Ancient Greek Horsemanship*. Berkeley: University of California, 1961.

Bingham, Woodbridge. *The Founding of the T'ang Dynasty*. Baltimore: Waverly Press, 1941.

Bandi, Hans-Georg, Henri Breuil, *et al*. *The Art of the Stone Age*. London: Methuen, 1961.

Barnett, R. D. *Assyrian Palace Reliefs and Their Influence on the Sculptures of Babylonia and Persia*. London: Batchworth Press, 1960.

Blackeagle, Joseph (Nez Perce). Interview, October 27, 1947.

Bolton, Herbert Eugene. *Rim of Christendom*: *A Biography of Eusebio Francisco Kino, Pacific Coast Pioneer*. New York: Macmillan, 1936.

——. *Spanish Explorations in the Southwest, 1542–1706*. New York: Macmillan, 1925.

Bowie, Beverley M. "The White Horses of Vienna," *National Geographic*, CXIV, No. 3 (September, 1958), pp. 401–419.

Burpee, Lawrence (ed.). *Journals and Letters of Pierre Gautier de Varennes de la Vérendrye and His Sons: With Correspondence between the Governors of Canada and the French Court, Touching the Search for the Western Sea*. Toronto: University of Toronto Press, 1927.

Cambridge Ancient History. 2nd ed., 12 vols. Cambridge and New York: Macmillan, 1928.

Chappell, Phil E. "History of the Missouri River," *Kansas Historical Collections*, IX (1905–1906), 237–316.

Chard, Thornton. "The Pinzgau Horse," *Western Horseman*, II, No. 5 (September–October, 1937), pp. 11.

Cox, Ross. *The Columbia River*. Edited with introduction by Edgar I. Stewart and Jane R. Stewart. Norman: University of Oklahoma Press, 1957.

Downes, James F. "The Origin and Spread of Riding in the Near East and Central Asia," *American Anthropologist*, LXIII (1961), 1193–1203.

Drury, E. M. *Henry Harmon Spalding*. Caldwell, Idaho: Caxton, 1936.

Ewers, John. *The Horse in Blackfoot Indian Culture*. Bureau of American Ethnology Bulletin 159, Smithsonian Institution, Washington, D. C., 1955.

Fairservis, Walter A., Jr. *The Ancient Kingdoms of the Nile*. New York: Crowell Company, 1962.

Falconer, Thomas: *On the Discovery of the Mississippi, and on the South-western, Oregon, and North-western Boundary of the United States. With a translation from the Original Manuscripts,*

Memoirs, etc., Relating to the Discovery of the Mississippi, by Robert Cavelier de la Salle and the Chevalier Henry de Tonty. London: 1844.

Ferguson, John C. "The Six Horses at the Tomb of the Emperor T'ai Tsung of the T'ang Dynasty." *Eastern Art,* III (1931), 61–71.

Firdausi. *Shah Namah.* Translated by A. G. and E. Warner. 9 vols. London: 1909–1925.

Haines, Francis. *The Nez Perces: Tribesmen of the Columbia Plateau.* Norman: University of Oklahoma Press, 1955.

———. "Where Did the Plains Indians Get Their Horses?", *American Anthropologist,* XL, No. 1 (January–March, 1938), 112–117.

———. "The Northward Spread of Horses among the Plains Indians," *American Anthropologist,* XL, No. 3 (July–September, 1938), pp. 429–437.

Hancar, Franz. *Das Pferd in Praehistorischer und Früher Historischer Zeit.* Wien: Verlag Herold, 1955.

Hendry, Anthony. *Journal, Proceedings and Transactions,* Royal Society of Canada, 3rd Series, I (1907), 329–351.

Herodotus. Translated by J. Enoch Powell. Oxford: Clarendon Press, 1949.

Hervey, John. *Racing in America, 1665–1865.* Privately printed by the Jockey Club of New York.

Jeffery, Andrew. Letter (December 13, 1947) to author from Department of Semitic Languages, Columbia University, New York City.

King, C. Harold. *A History of Civilization.* New York: Charles Scribner's Sons, 1956.

Kroeber, A. L. *Anthropology.* Revised edition. New York: Harcourt Brace & Co., 1948.

Kurth, Betty. *Die Deutschen Bilderpiche des Mittelalters.* Wien: 1926.

Lawton, Thomas. Letter (July 26, 1962) to author, from Cambridge, Massachusetts.

Le Vavasseur, Colonel. Letter (May 8, 1947) to author, from Casablanca, Morocco.

Lewis, Charles. Letter (May 8, 1947) to author, from U. S. Consulate, Casablanca, Morocco.

Lewis, William S., and Paul C. Phillips (eds.). *The Journal of John Work.* SEE Work, John.

Lhote, Henri. *The Search for the Tassili Frescoes.* New York: E. P. Dutton & Co., 1959.

Life Magazine, XXVI, No. 4 (January 24, 1949).

Llewellyn, Bart., Sir Phys. "The British Spotted Horse," *Riding* (October 1949).

Lowie, Robert H. *Indians of the Plains.* New York: McGraw-Hill, 1954.

Lubbock, Francis Richard. *Six Decades in Texas or Memoirs of Francis Richard Lubbock, Governor of Texas in War-time, 1861–1863.* Austin: Ben C. Jones & Co., Printers, 1900.

Margry, Pierre. *Memoires et documents pour servir a l'histoire des origines francaises des pays d'outre-mer. Découvertes et établissements des Francais dans l'ouest et dans le sud de l'Amerique Septentrionale (1614–1754).* 6 vols. Paris: 1879–1888.

Niles Weekly Register, XVI, No. 23 (July 31, 1819), 377.

Olmstead, A. T. *History of Assyria.* Chicago: University of Chicago Press, 1960.

———. *History of the Persian Empire.* Chicago: University of Chicago Press, 1948.

Pan Kuh. *The History of the Former Han Dynasty.* Translated by Homer H. Dubs. 2 vols. Baltimore: Waverly Press, 1944.

Pacific Railway Survey Reports. 12 vols. Washington, D. C.: Government Printing Office, 1860.

Peake, Harold, and Herbert John Fleure. *The Steppe and the Sown.* Vol. V of *Corridors of Time.* New Haven: Yale University Press, 1928.

Pedersen, Aksel. *Knabstruppere.* A pamphlet prepared by the Livestock Commission, Braureige, Denmark, 1958.

Persian Literature. Translated by James Atkinson. 2 vols., rev.

edition, *World's Greatest Literature*. New York: P. F. Collier and Son, 1900.

Rice, Tamara Talbot. *The Scythians*. London: Thames & Hudson, 1957.

Ross, Alexander. *Adventures of the First Settlers on the Oregon or Columbia River*. Vol. VII in *Early Western Travels*. Edited by Reuben Gold Thwaites. Cleveland: Arthur H. Clark, 1904.

Ross, Marvin C. *The West of Alfred Jacob Miller*. Norman: University of Oklahoma Press, 1951.

Sarciat, Pedro A. *El Pelo Yaquane en el Caballo Criollo*. Buenos Aires: Ferrari Bros., 1940.

Scholes, F. V. "Troublous Times in New Mexico, 1659–1670," *New Mexico Historical Review*, XII (1937), 134–174.

Schulman, Alan Richard. "Egyptian Representations of Horsemen and Riding in the New Kingdom," *Journal of Near Eastern Studies*, XVI (January–October, 1957), pp. 263–271.

Sitwell, Sacheverell. *The Hunters and the Hunted*. New York: Macmillan, 1948.

Spinden, Herbert J. "Nez Perce Tales," *Journal of American Folk-lore*, XXI (1908), p. 158.

Stein, Aurel. *Innermost Asia*. 4 vols. Oxford: Clarendon Press, 1928.

Strabo. *Geography*. Translated by H. C. Hamilton and W. Falconer. 3 vols. New York: Bell, 1889–1903.

Swindler, Mary Hamilton. *Ancient Painting*. New Haven: Yale University Press, 1929.

Tarn, W. W. *The Greeks in Bactria and India*. Cambridge: Cambridge University Press, 1951.

———. *Hellenistic Military and Naval Developments*. Cambridge: Cambridge University Press, 1930.

Textilwerk, Das. Introduction by Ernest Flemming. Berlin: 1927.

Thomas, A.B. "Spanish Expeditions Northeast of New Mexico." Unpublished Ph.D. dissertation, University of California, 1928.

Thwaites, Reuben Gold (ed.) *The Original Journals of the Lewis and Clark Expedition, 1804–1806*. 8 vols. New York: 1904–1906.

United States Secretary of War. *Report*, 1877.

Von Shinkel, Diana. Letter (August 5, 1958) to author from Hallansberg, Moholen, Sweden.

Waley, Arthur. "The Heavenly Horses of Fergana," *History Today*, Vol. V (February, 1955), pp. 95–103.

Watson, Burton. *Records of the Grand Historian of China*. 2 vols. New York: Columbia University Press, 1961.

Weibel, Adele Coulin. *Two Thousand Years of Textiles*. New York: Pantheon, 1952.

White, Charles William. *Tomb Tile Pictures of Ancient China*. Toronto: University of Toronto Press, 1939.

Windisch-Graetz, Mathilde. *The Spanish Riding School*. New York: A. S. Barnes & Co., 1957.

Work, John. *The Journal of John Work*. Edited by William S. Lewis and Paul C. Phillips. Vol. I, *Early Western Journals*. Cleveland: Arthur H. Clark, 1923.

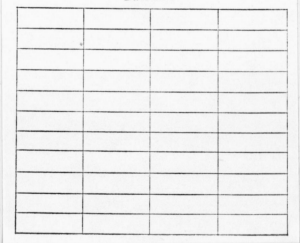